The Creatives: Leadership

I0554702

Yvette C. Owens
2X International Best-Selling Author

Legal Disclaimer

Connect with MPowered Voice Publishing
www.MPoweredvoicepublishing.ca

Table of Contents

Contents

Dedication

To my beloved parents, Donald and Collen Cary:

Thank you for the unwavering commitment to integrity, accuracy, respect, and kindness you instilled in me from a young age. Your tireless efforts to maintain a good reputation and name in the community were worthwhile, and I am grateful for the high standard of leadership that you modeled for me.

Growing up in a well-respected family, it would have been easy to believe we could do whatever we wanted without consequences. But you taught us that our actions mattered and that we were responsible for upholding the legacy that you had worked so hard to build.

I will never forget the times you worked with students to help them become their best selves or the love you showed to the orphaned young man who lived with us, even when he made mistakes. Your compassion and generosity have impacted me, and I strive to emulate those qualities.

I am also grateful for the gift of music that you shared with our family. Your passion for music and how you used it to bring joy and inspiration to others was truly remarkable. I will always treasure the memories of performing alongside you in concerts and musical events.

Thank you for being such wonderful parents and role models. I am honored to be your child, and I hope to continue to make you proud of how I live my life.

With love and admiration,

Yvette

Foreword

The Creatives: Leadership was inspired by the high standard of leadership that was modeled for Yvette C. Owens by her amazing and beloved parents in her home. She was blessed to have a great start to her life THE RIGHT WAY!

I believe Yvette discovered the importance of patience in leadership, not only in her senior role as a leader but also in birthing this book. The right to change your mind was another virtue uncovered as well along the way. Writing a book strengthens one's energy and character; growth is inescapable as it calls for going into the depths of the soul where no man/woman has yet been!

Leadership is a wonderful playground where you are faced with your strengths and weaknesses. Is it Egoship or leadership? Educational Leadership? Kingdom Leadership? or is it Radical Dreaming? It is not always what people imagine it to be. Leadership is about serving and not being served.

Yvette C. Owens is a true inspiration to her teams as well as leaders alike. This book will allow you to go deep within and look at your own leadership skills and weaknesses, as there is always room for improvement. It will both enlighten and inspire you to be a stronger leader in your workplace, community, home, and family.

God is always our internal leader, and our role is to sharpen our hearing!

LOVE AND LIGHT

Marianne Padjan

Introduction

We are introducing "T*he Creatives: Leadership*" - a powerful guide to creating healthy, thriving cultures in the workplace, ministry, and the community.

For author Yvette C. Owens, leadership is not just a job title - it's a calling. With a deep-seated faith in God and a commitment to living purpose on purpose, Yvette has overcome tremendous obstacles to become an authentic creative leader.

In "*The Creatives: Leadership*," Yvette and her friends and colleagues, The Creatives, share the insights and strategies that have helped them to navigate the challenges of leadership with grace, resilience, and compassion. Drawing on their experiences of overcoming life challenges, inequities, injustices, and abuse, the authors offer a roadmap for creating a healthy culture that is innovative, creative, and profitable for all.

Through inspiring stories and practical advice, *The Creatives: Leadership* shows how true win-wins are possible when leaders prioritize the well-being and growth of their team members. The authors offer tools for building trust, fostering collaboration, and promoting creativity, all while remaining firmly rooted in godly principles.

Whether you're a seasoned leader or just starting on your leadership journey, "*The Creatives: Leadership*" is an essential guide for anyone who wants to create a healthy, thriving workplace, ministry, or community culture. Join Yvette and The Creatives on this transformative journey towards becoming a creative leader and unlock your team's potential to achieve extraordinary things.

Yvette C. Owens

Unleashing the Power of Creativity in Leadership

Yvette C. Owens

Effective leadership requires more than traditional management skills in today's rapidly evolving business landscape. As corporate leaders, you face the challenge of engaging your teams, fostering creativity, and driving high performance while increasing loyalty to your organization's vision and boosting revenue. This chapter will explore the essential elements of leadership that enable creativity to flourish, allowing you to build high-performing teams that thrive in the face of challenges. By embracing these principles, you can unleash the collective creative genius within your organization and create a culture of innovation and success.

My Why:

During my 25th year in corporate, I hit a season of challenges to my career, reputation, and my teams' abilities to complete their assignments. It was a succession of all hell breaking loose. There was a trend of valuable information being withheld. Unrealistic timelines were set along with receiving increased work. I would ask my leadership for help, and too often, the response was, "Just keep doing what you're doing." The problem is that our path needed to yield the results we needed. Our customers were asking questions that we couldn't answer. We were boxed in on every side and set up for failure. Before this period, the teams were very successful. What changed? To this day, I am still waiting for an official answer. I know within my soul that someone somewhere decided that the structure of the organization needed to change, and the approach was to disband teams to make way for a new direction. I am not questioning the need to adjust a business model. Change is the only constant we can depend on. I ask how it was handled poorly, messing with people's reputations and credibility. Creative leadership is essential to satisfy business goals while protecting individuals during transitions, even when some individuals or teams must be let go. Integrity and transparency always lead to healthy relationships when difficult decisions are required.

I lost my joy trying to adhere to practices that did not serve me in the long run. Following the game plan, mastering the language, and continuously ranking as a high performer did not protect me and my teams from downsizing, and in the process, we had to fight to maintain our dignity. The hurt and disappointment we experienced impacted my group and those watching the scenarios unfold. Loyalty and engagement plummeted. The indirect message sent across the organization was that leadership did not value the high-performers, so anyone could suffer the demise of the next business decision without considering the people involved and who serve the company well. Have you experienced a similar situation? It just isn't fair, but it is too often a reality.

A Cry for Creative Leadership:

Organizations must be careful to avoid mishandling individuals invested in the success of the vision. It is too costly, especially in an era where people know they have plenty of choices to serve and grow in environments that meet most of their needs. Individuals no longer have to settle, suck it up, or compromise. The possibilities are endless, from an increasing array of organizations willing to tailor onboarding packages to entrepreneurship. Let's vow to make decisions that serve the entire culture. Let's value every person we invite to join us on the journey to fulfill our vision and goals. It is time for actual open-door policies refusing to allow egos to rule. Our products, services, movements, and ministries are needed. However, consumers and clients make conscious decisions on where to purchase based on the beliefs and practices of organizations' leadership. Consider the following five (5) recommendations to fortify your performance and effectiveness to accelerate your success exponentially in this fast-paced climate. Let's vow to be genuinely successful on all fronts.

Defying Traditional Notions of Leadership:

Leadership is not simply a position bestowed upon the oldest or most experienced individual. True leaders emerge by answering questions, fulfilling needs, providing direction, and rallying people around a cause or vision. It is the ability to inspire, encourage, and challenge others to think beyond their comfort zones and achieve better results. Creativity often thrives when leaders are willing to venture into uncharted territory, clean up messes, and pave new paths. As a leader, you must cultivate a mindset that values creativity and embraces the contributions of every individual.

Embracing Collaboration and Diverse Perspectives:

The wisdom of a leader lies not in having all the answers but in recognizing the power of collaboration. Engaging your team's expertise and encouraging diverse perspectives can lead to far better solutions than any individual could achieve alone. Foster an environment where healthy thinking, speaking, and challenges are welcomed and expected. Innovative leaders seek to combine their expertise with that of others, creating a collective brilliance that fuels success.

Navigating Adversity and Upholding Team Integrity:

Leadership is tested during adversity. When your team faces challenges, rallying together and protecting their progress and reputation is crucial. Define the landscape and framework for your team, removing obstacles and keeping them informed of changes that may impact their journey. Grant them the freedom to work within these parameters, and collective brilliance will emerge.

However, remember that every contribution is personal to the individual making it, and treating their efforts lightly can lead to demotivation and diminished commitment. As a leader, it is essential to strengthen your diplomacy skills, calling out the truth when critical resources or information are lacking and representing your team in the face of adversity.

Celebrate Contributions:

Monetary rewards alone are not enough to acknowledge and appreciate your team's efforts. Sharing the team's success with senior leadership and publicly recognizing individual achievements can create a culture where team members actively seek ways to contribute to the team's victories. When the team wins, everyone wins. By building an environment that values and celebrates the contributions of each team member, you foster loyalty, increase engagement, and boost overall performance.

Building a Safe Zone for Creativity:

To unleash the full potential of creativity, leaders must create a safe and supportive environment. Every safe, collaborative environment requires certain key elements. It must be:

Bias-Free:

Check your assumptions and allow your beliefs to be proven or challenged. Avoid letting even the slightest bias derail the group's collective efforts. Embrace diverse perspectives and recognize the transformative power they can bring.

Empowering Every Individual:

Be direct and repetitive in calling out everyone's expertise and holding them accountable for showing up as the best selves in their respective roles. Cultivate an expectation that everyone's contribution is valuable and necessary for the team's success.

Supporting:

Pay attention to the needs of your team and be prepared to step in and cover for a teammate in emergencies. This level of support goes beyond understanding technical skills; it means being able to temporarily fill in gaps, maintain momentum, and ask relevant questions to move the team forward.

Championing and Celebrating:

Regularly champion and celebrate your team, considering each individual's unique preferences. Acknowledging their contributions in meaningful ways creates an atmosphere where creativity thrives, and team members are motivated to help the team win.

Protecting the Collective Creative Genius:

Act as a buffer to shield your team from abuse and exploitation of their expertise. Evaluate requests for assistance carefully, considering the impact on your team's workload and ensuring their contributions are respected. Be a wise partner, advocating for proper involvement and resource allocation.

Conclusion:

By embracing the principles outlined in this chapter, corporate leaders can unlock the true potential of their teams. Building a culture that nurtures creativity, fosters collaboration, and values individual contributions will lead to high-performing teams, increased loyalty, and enhanced revenue. As leaders, you have the power to shape an environment where creativity flourishes, enabling your organization to tackle new challenges, drive innovation, and deliver exceptional products and services. Embrace the role of a creative leader and watch your team's potential soar.

Yvette C. Owens

Yvette is a speaker, international best-selling author, leadership coach, and consultant, who empowers leaders to lead with their soul and create a thriving culture for all. She guides leaders on how to lean into the resistance during times of change. By embracing this resistance, we unlock the potential for our teams to not only accept change but to invest in it wholeheartedly. Yvette teaches change leadership principles to increase adoption, retain talent, and build high-performing teams using the proprietary V.I.C.T.O.R. framework Yvette, aka Changologist, is a board-certified change management professional (A.C.M.P.). She has 40+ years of sharing her vibrant resilience, compassion, and influence in teaching "Dealing With Resistance To Accept And Invest In Change" during keynote speeches and live and virtual working sessions.

Contact Information:

Email: VisionToReality@DestinySpeak.com

LinkedIn:
https://www.linkedin.com/in/yvettecowensbusinessambassador/

Website: DestinySpeak Leadership & Organization Development Company

Becoming a Servant Leader

Jose Escobar

"Servant leadership is all about making the goals clear, and doing whatever it takes to help people win. In that situation, they don't work for you; you work for them."

- Ken Blanchard, American business consultant, author, and speaker

Ever since the dawn of history, leadership has been the largest single factor that has had a transcendent impact on society. In many places around the world, innovation, inventions, and progress have flourished due to solid leadership. By the same token, in many places around the world, innovation, inventions, and progress have been stifled by poor leadership. In this regard, the quality of leadership over a community, society and nation has far-reaching repercussions on how society either progresses or falls into oblivion and anarchy.

History is filled with great and infamous leaders who have had a tremendous share of impact. The list is inexhaustible, but it includes, among others, Jesus Christ, Confucius, George Washington, Abraham Lincoln, Napoleon, Alexander the Great, Julius Caesar, Henry Ford, Thomas A. Edison, Martin Luther King Jr. and many others. All these leaders have had an unforgettable impact on the landscape of history.

I'm not a stranger to leadership. I've been in leadership roles for a long time, from branch management in the banking world to the insurance business selling life insurance, then the property and casualty space. Eventually, I became the Sales Director for a global martial arts company, *Educational Funding Company* (EFC). After all these diverse and dynamic experiences, I eventually started my own businesses which include the *Connected Leaders Academy* and *The Entrepreneur's Bookshelf*. As John Maxwell says, *"Leadership is influence,"* right? So, I want to really make sure my chapter speaks to the power of influencing others into their best selves, into their higher calling and into their full potential.

Leaders have to be exemplary. We have to be in the trenches and on the front lines. I believe as leaders, we don't just speak from the pulpit or, you know, as they say, "the sage from the stage," right? We have to be in the battle with those we serve and show people how to get things done. We show people what hard work is. We show people what discipline looks like. We show people what having faith looks like. We show people what commitment is all about. That's the basis of the essence of leadership for me. I've been privileged to experience leadership on a lot of levels in my life.

The first place where I witnessed leadership in action was in my household growing up. My parents Raul and Gloria Escobar have been married for 49 years, going on 50. I think this December 2023, it'll be 50 years since they got married, and they have been happily married, although they've had ups and downs like any marriage. There's no such thing as a perfect marriage, yet I've witnessed both my parents exude high-level leadership.

My dad always led as the head of our household growing up. He had multiple jobs and never made excuses not to show up for the family. He would cater to my mother on every level with a deep love that is so admirable. My dad always knew the line between disciplining us kids and mentorship. He showed up strong in his day jobs which ultimately led him to get promoted all the time.

He started out in this country as a dishwasher and also building homes in construction, all the way up to every single position you can think of in the restaurant business, to the point where he ended up owning a couple of restaurants. My mother also had a strong work ethic as she came to this country and started cleaning multiple homes, to the tune of three to four homes daily.

Eventually, my mom started a business called *Jafra Cosmetics*. She never allowed herself to become complacent and just go through the motions in life. She built this business on the side little by little. In due time it grew to a nationwide company where she was mentoring hundreds of women to achieve success as well. Her business grew massively, and she became a phenomenal leader.

She became this leader that she didn't realize she always was, and she was leading all kinds of women all around the country, going to seminars, speaking from stages, getting awards and creating massive impact. My dad also helped her do a lot of training seminars for her organization and various things to help her build her business.

Their story is quite inspirational. They left their native country of Guatemala to arrive in the USA in their early twenties with little money, no English and little education to build an empire, living the American dream and buying a million-dollar home as well as retiring relatively young. Now, they're living life on their terms, doing their thing after leaving a trail of tremendous impact along the way. I grew up watching real leadership in my own home. I am very grateful for my parents and all they have taught me along the journey of life. I am living my dream today, building my own empire in business, largely in part due to the leadership I learned from them.

I have been blessed to have many great mentors pour into my life. Chris Cherest is one of them. I met him in Amway (it used to be called Quixtar when I joined) back when I was only eighteen years old. He taught me so many powerful golden nuggets on sales and leadership. I cannot begin to express my gratitude for him in my life. He helped me so much and certainly didn't have to. It's fair to say I kind of fell into my mother's footsteps, and that led to a lot of wonderful growth in terms of business development. Dr. Arlene and Dr. Lennard George have also been instrumental mentors in my life that have strengthened my leadership journey. They actually were the ones who introduced me to Chris Cherest. Dr. Mel Davis has also played a key role in my personal development and leadership over the years. I had some dark times in my life, and Mel was there to lead me through. I even hired some "expensive" coaches like Tai Lopez and Richard Yu as well, among many others. So, I've had a lot of great coaches and mentors and leaders pour into my life, and that helped me learn what leadership is all about and then of course, I was put in positions to lead. You'll be surprised that when you're thrown into the deep end of the ocean when it comes to business and life, you're going to have to learn how to swim real quick, or you'll drown.

I am not a highly educated person (in terms of college), but I have a high emotional quotient (EQ), high-level work ethic and am very coachable. I always was able to land jobs that require college degrees. I sold my way into these positions with just my personality and my sales ability. As I say, winners always find a way to win.

When I was put in leadership roles, I had to figure out how to figure it out, how to get it done and that's really what helped me in a lot of ways. I am very resourceful and make no excuses. Over time, I realized that I developed into a great leader. This put a desire in me to now help develop other leaders too. There's this great book called *"Leading Leaders to Leadership."* I believe in that mission. So, I think we all have a certain level of leadership within us. A lot of times, we just have to be in a position to lead, and when we have that chance to lead, we have to give it all we have.

When the time comes to lead, it's going to require a few things like hard work, commitment, discipline, dedication and laser focus. All of the key things that most people aren't willing to do, which is why most people are not leaders. The people who lead are the ones who are willing to put in those extra efforts because the extra efforts are the ingredients that make leadership extraordinary. We're all ordinary, and extraordinary just means you're putting in that little extra, and that extra is the discipline, the hard work, the long hours, not complaining, removing excuses and, of course, mental toughness. As leaders, we have to take extreme ownership. Ownership is huge. Jocko Willink wrote a great book called "*Extreme Ownership.*" If someone had success under your leadership, it's okay to take a sliver of credit (given you helped on some level). If someone fails to get a job done under your leadership, then you must own it all, one hundred percent of that failure should fall on the leader, period.

Ultimately, strive to become the best servant leader you can because that's the kind of leadership that impacts people and communities. Use your circumstances, experiences, and background as your leadership USP (Unique Selling Proposition) and find creative ways to become an impactful leader in life, drawing from the depths of your soul. The world today needs you to lead. Take on the challenge to step into the servant leader that lies within you.

Jose Escobar

Jose is an award-winning, nationally recognized personal development speaker, eight-time published author, sales professional, husband and father of five children. He leads compelling high-level communities consisting of entrepreneurs and advanced leaders through two multi-six-figure business models, *The Entrepreneur's Bookshelf* and the *Connected Leaders Academy*.

Jose's magnetic personality shines in his presentations, where he has reached audiences collectively over 30 million and radiates throughout his dynamic coaching programs, inspiring his international 300+ entrepreneur and executive clientele to master their personal and professional excellence. His past sales experience led him to amass over $29 million in revenue for the companies he served, and this family man's sales and coaching in the martial arts industry has positively affected the lives of over 500 thousand families for the better. Learn more about Jose's products and services at

www.TheEntrepreneursBookshelf.com

Contact Information:

jaesco25@gmail.com

301-944-4755 - cell phone

.

Lead the Way You Want People to Follow

Katrice Cornett

Being a leader is not as easy as some people make it look. It can be very challenging, but also rewarding at times. While writing this chapter, I realized that most of the leadership positions I have been in weren't even something that I sought. I never really thought of myself as a leader, but somehow, I found myself in this position more times than I can count. What I do know about myself is that I am a person who likes to do things with excellence. I believe that I am a natural-born fixer and a problem solver. I often find myself thinking of and observing things that seem very obvious to me, but most people tend to overlook and understand what the solution should be.

I'd like to bring to your attention three qualities I think a creative leader naturally possesses. **The first quality is an undeniable ability to pay attention to the small things** as well as things that go unnoticed. This is where my creativity begins. In this situation, the creative leader sees what is missing from what is already there. I know it sounds crazy, but most people are functioning below what they are really capable of. It takes a creative leader to recognize the gifts and talents in the people around them and come up with creative ways to get them to recognize that they exist. Once you have creatively achieved this goal it then becomes essential to show them how what they bring to the table is important to the success of the company and/or project.

I find that being a creative leader is not something that I can't really turn off. Even when I am not the leader in a situation, on a project or event, it is natural for me to assess a situation and come up with creative ways to make it better. I have no problem with leading from the back. This is actually my preferred way to lead. When I am in the back, I can see the full picture much clearer. Working with the team and being in the trenches with them is when some of my greatest ideas come to me. When we, as leaders, understand that we are only as strong and/or successful as our weakest link, we become great. And get this, when you discover the person and/or thing that is causing the project to be off course, instead of looking to get rid of the thing, we reassess, reaffirm, and get creative with ways to get them or it is moving in the right direction. I am a firm believer that even something that looks like it doesn't fit can add value and it might just surprise you.

Creative leadership will put you in a position where you will be all alone. Because I see things from a totally different perspective, people don't always get my vision right away. Usually, it is those close to me, the people who I think should know me the best, that don't see it and may sometimes cast doubt and unbelief as to the validity of the idea. Nevertheless, as a creative leader, I have learned to stay the course and not allow the opinions of others to discourage me from my goals. They eventually come around.

This leads me to the second quality I believe a creative leader should possess. The ability to lead from the second seat.

You do not have to be the CEO or the President of a company to be a creative leader. To me, it actually takes more creativity to lead from the second seat. As an administrative assistant for over 30 years, it took great imagination and creativity to organize and support(lead) my department.

I speak about it later in the chapter, but I was an Office Manager who had the privilege of servicing approximately 2000 people during the course of a calendar school year. It takes a massive amount of creativity to implement policies and procedures that are put in place by Supervisors and Administrators who have certain goals that they are trying to obtain but, at the same time, do not understand the dynamics of what you are working with on your level. How do you stay in good standing with your boss while trying to make sure that everyone else's needs, which you directly service every day, are met? Creative leadership is my answer.

There is no way I am going to alienate my direct co-workers, so I have to figure out how to make this directive suit the team. I refer to this as my creative workaround. I am going to come up with something so creative that it allows me to help my superiors reach their goals and, at the same time, allows my team to understand that I have their backs. Here is an example of how I did that.

Example: As the Office Manager for the Child Study Team of a large high school population where a team of 5 case managers, 8 guidance counselors, 4 vice-principals and 33 teachers are servicing approximately 500 to 750, sometimes 1000 students, I was responsible for coordinating meetings that encompassed all of the above personnel. Most of the school year, it was from month to month on the anniversary date of a meeting they had three years prior. However, once a year, it was the entire special education student body, and the time frame always overlapped with some of the 3-year meetings.

The state has mandates that have to be met in a certain timeframe, or the school will get penalized. My first year of doing this was really confusing and antiquated because our computer software was not equipped to handle an automated process. This I could not control. I would bring work home and have my children help me, and that all worked fine until I started getting complaints about teachers not attending meetings because they did not know that they were scheduled to come. This frustrated me because, at that point, I was walking schedules to their mailboxes and putting them in there myself. Why they were not receiving them was beyond me, but I had no proof of this process.

The third quality I believe a creative leader should possess is positivity and not being easily swayed

I mentioned earlier in the chapter that being a creative leader can become lonely. Being lonely can sometimes cause depression or even a negative mindset. When you find yourself in this space, you must be able to fight with a positive reaction. There have been many times that I'm in a space where I don't feel like the best version of myself, but I keep moving. I make positive declarations to myself, and I keep at it until I can get back on track. So, I'm not saying that those feelings won't come; what I am saying is a creative leader cannot give in to them. We are a unique breed, and what we have created is unique. When creative leaders are strong enough to see it through, we will be the solution to someone's problem.

What I find is most of my creative moments are tied to some type of strong emotion that I am dealing with, and it isn't always positive. As an independent recording artist, most of my greatest songs have been created during times of great challenges in my life. What if I had curled up in my bed? I wouldn't have been able to create great songs for the Kingdom, such as *"Forever God Reigns,"* *"Blessed is the Name of Jesus,"* *"Grace & Favor,"* *"Strong & Courageous,"* and the list goes on.

A creative leader should understand that greatness comes with a cost, but you can't let it break you. This is one of the most important lessons I have learned on this journey of creative leadership. I'd like to just conclude by sharing some of the many opportunities I have had in my life and how creative leadership has been and is something that I value and use.

Below I have written a brief summary of key roles I have held in my life and how creative leadership allowed me to be successful in each of them. As a child, I was exposed to all forms of creative expression. My parents are 'creatives.' so I was in plays, musicals, performing concerts, took piano and voice lessons, and learned to crochet, do needlepoint, and macrame. I was taught that there is no limit to what I can do as a creative and that I should be using my creative abilities for the glory of God. This has not only shaped my thinking, but it has become the very essence of who I am.

As a mother and wife, it was challenging at times but being 'a creative' helped me to come up with different ways to manage our budget, shop and provide for our family and to keep things moving forward through good and bad times. Sometimes I don't even think my children realized that we were not rich. They never missed a meal, and they always had a roof over their heads. It was not always easy, but being able to think outside of the box enabled me to make it look like it was.

As an employee of the Board of Education in Atlantic City, NJ, I was the first person to be hired in the position of Child Study Team Secretary for the high school. This was really interesting because I had to develop the department's office policies and procedures from scratch. My creative skills really came in handy here. Creating templates, operating procedures for staff and students, as well as daily routines to help keep the workflow productive and efficient, was one of my greatest career achievements in that position.

It has been my absolute pleasure sharing my thoughts, experiences and even some practical information with you about creative leadership.

Katrice Cornett

Katrice is the CEO/Founder of *HP Visual Connections/ Entertainment*, a business that was created to market and promote her gospel recording ministry.

Over the years, Katrice has served as a Worship Leader, Music and Choir Director, Vocal Coach, Musician and Consultant to various churches throughout the states of New Jersey, Pennsylvania, and Connecticut.

Katrice is the State Coordinator for *David's Tent NJ,* which is a movement of Worship unto our Lord and Savior Jesus Christ that was established in 2011 in Washington DC and is now happening in ALL 50 states.

As a Contemporary Praise & Worship Recording artist Katrice has been able to bless listeners throughout the world. Katrice has been set apart by God to help empower churches, music ministries, and congregations to understand how to intentionally worship Jesus with pure hearts and clean hands.

Katrice's faith in God and her strong belief in the Word have kept her focused and determined to share Christ with the world through her music. Katrice believes that only what you do for Christ will last. She lives her life in accordance with Colossians 3:23-24

"Whatever you do, work at it with all your heart, as working for the Lord, not for human masters, since you know that you will receive an inheritance from the Lord as a reward. It is the Lord Christ you are serving."

Email: kcornett@hpvisualconnections.net

Facebook @KatriceCornett7 & @HPVisualConnect |

LinkedIn @https://www.linkedin.com/in/kcornett45

The Making of a Creative Leader

Donna Carter

When I think about creative leadership, I immediately reflect on the leaders I had and what I learned from each of them. Because my leadership reflects my experiences and leadership that helped me to thrive as well as the leaders who did not. All these combined experiences helped me and continue to help me lead creatively and recognize the responsibility that comes with leading. This list includes so many individuals, not just in my professional life but in my personal life as well. There is no way I could even begin this discussion without acknowledging my parents, who taught me how to lead with excellence and integrity even when no one is watching. I can remember my father saying, "Remember you represent the Cary name (my maiden name)." There was a time when that felt like a huge burden, but now I can look at that statement, what it instilled in me and be thankful and appreciative for what it led me to accomplish.

There are a few key factors that accompany my ability to lead creatively. **The first factors are my relationship with and faith in God.** Because my faith in God is a foundational pillar, and I desire to be in right standing with Him, I will admit mistakes, give credit to team members, and strive to lead with integrity and vulnerability. Do I always get it right? No. However, it is the desire to be pleasing in His sight that helps me admit when I get it wrong, go back and try to make things right, continually examine myself and acknowledge when I am coming from places of frustration or anger. It is His love for me, that allows me to love others and the fact that I am in relationship with Him, helps me honor my commitments, and put forth my best effort regardless. I used to think it was my great work ethic, but when I look back over my career, I understand that it is my love for Him that keeps me performing at a high level, even when I was not getting recognized, appreciated or paid my worth. It was the trust in Him and that He fights my battles for me that has allowed me to lead with passion and a commitment to excellence even when leaders over me were not always leading in that same manner. The creativity in my leadership has always been connected to Jesus and His power that lives within me.

The second factor in leading creatively is learning how to sit with my own discomfort.

Before I define what this means to me, I want to share what it takes for me to sit with my own discomfort. First, I need to be self-aware enough to know what makes me uncomfortable, acknowledge when the discomfort arises and be willing to explore the "why" behind the discomfort. Often, we think the discomfort is coming from external factors, but if we look deep enough and get honest with ourselves, the discomfort is usually coming from within. Knowing when I am getting uncomfortable and then remembering that my team member's or colleague's growth and development are more important than my discomfort. The discomfort of my vulnerability is not as important as being honest with the individuals I lead. For example, there was an incident when a few individuals on my team thought a staff member was not ready for a particular role. They came to me and stated their case and thought it would not turn out well if this individual was placed in the role. The team had a pretty good case; they felt like the individual was misleading on some paperwork, which would disqualify them from the role and be disruptive to the team. While the team made a valid argument, I saw no reason not to believe the individual and thought it would be risky to question the individual's paperwork. So, I informed them that, in all fairness, we have no proof to the contrary and to give the individual a chance. So, we did. It did not turn out well. Within a short time frame, the individual violated policy, and we had to remove them from the role. While I don't think I would have changed my decision with the evidence presented, I did go back to the team and their team members, who were impacted, and apologized while acknowledging that their immediate leadership thought this would be problematic and I was the final decision maker that allowed the disruption. This was important for several reasons, I did not want the credibility of the team leaders to be impacted, and their staff needed to know that they were thoughtful about building the team and the decision-making process. I also wanted to take responsibility for my decision. I am not sure if that is creative as much as it is the right thing to do. Was it uncomfortable? Yes. Did I have thoughts on what it would look like to the team? Yes. Even after I did it, did I second guess how I was perceived? Yes. But at the end of the day, my discomfort is second to the development of my team and walking in integrity.

The third factor is the ability to receive feedback.

This should be a no-brainer; however, it is not always as easy as it sounds. As a leader, I must be open to feedback from peers, colleagues, direct reports, and so many others. Creative leadership provides brave spaces for individuals to feel comfortable sharing their thoughts, expressing if something about an individual's leadership style makes them uncomfortable and providing innovative thought feedback. Perhaps there is a better way to perform a function or manage a process. This is creative and helps develop critical thinking skills within organizations. Individuals are inspired and much more productive when they know that their thoughts and contributions will be heard and considered. I challenge you to think about the first word that comes to mind when you hear the word "feedback". Do you think of words like growth, development, opportunity and thankful? Or do you think about words like conflict, punitive, hard, avoidance or judgement? How we view feedback as individuals will determine how we utilize and manage feedback conversations as leaders. This also goes back to learning to sit with your own discomfort. Giving difficult feedback can be as difficult as receiving it. But as a leader, a wife, mother, and a friend it is more important for me to share the difficult feedback so the issue can be corrected or resolved than it is for me to avoid the discomfort of the conversation. When I choose my own comfort or my own fears over the opportunity to share difficult feedback, and I have done that, I am doing a disservice to that individual and making assumptions about their ability to receive instruction and/or their desire to change.

The last factor I would like to discuss is a combination of the ability to listen and allow your team to shine.

The listening part took me a while to learn, and I think I am a better listener today, but still learning. Listening and being present in meetings and your one-on-one time with your direct reports is so very important. Keeping your individual meetings with your team and not continually cancelling and rescheduling is also important. Trust me, they know when you are not present, and as a human resource professional, one of the main complaints I hear is, "My leader never has one-on-one meetings with me." or "The one-on-one meetings are on the calendar, but we have only had two all year." We will make time for what we prioritize. So, I will leave that there. A lot of times in corporate settings, the loudest voice gets the attention. There is little room for the quiet thinker in most board rooms and leadership conversations. I have learned and become very comfortable with only speaking if I have something to contribute, a valid question or just something to say. I do not have to be the loudest person in the room, nor do I always have to be in the front. Creative leaders build up their teams and develop them so that they can facilitate the presentation. They can manage situations and provide their team members with exposure. We often negate the importance of exposure, but it is extremely important. How often have you been in a discussion with a group of leaders discussing succession, and great individuals are being overlooked only because they have not been provided the right exposure to the decision-makers? This is a time when creative leaders will advocate for those individuals who are not in the room, but that is a chapter

~ 30 ~

by itself. Creative leadership listens to their team and looks for opportunities to provide them exposure to key stakeholders that allows them to shine. Creative leaders will prepare their team members for that exposure and help them maneuver the cultural and political landscape of the organization. I will add that no matter how great your organization is, there is a political landscape to maneuver. Leaders in my life who helped me maneuver and prepare for meetings with certain stakeholders so I could be successful are the leaders I continue to stay in touch with, and I can tell you their names. Why? Because my success was their success, because they saw something in me that I did not always see in myself, they told me the truth even when it hurt, and they wanted me to succeed. I could tell that they truly wanted me to succeed, and I am forever thankful to each of them.

Creative leaders are continually growing. I say that because I am continually growing. These leaders have a desire for self-development and learning. At first, I was going to say professional development, but when I think about it, it goes beyond professional development. We cannot separate our leadership from who we are as a person; it does not work that way. We may be able to function that way for a while, but it is not sustainable. Creative leaders must learn how to be self-led first and be willing to do the personal work to be able to understand their own strengths, weaknesses, discomforts, fears, and so on. Because without that continual self-reflection, leaders have the propensity to do harm to the individuals that they lead. For me, creative leadership means getting up every day, renewing my mind through prayer and time with God, and making a very conscious decision to self-reflect and be aware of my actions, words, and impact on those who cross my path. Approaching conflict with curiosity and compassion and doing the sometimes-hard work of holding space for those individuals I lead, partner with and support.

Donna Carter

Donna Carter lives in Kentucky, outside of Lexington, with her husband of 22 years and teenage daughter. She loves the Lord and strives to put Him first. She has been working in human resources for 20 years, which includes global leadership, developing organizational strategy and DEIB initiatives. Her career includes serving as the human resource leadership in K-12 education, government, manufacturing, and medical industries.

She recently founded and organized the *Clark County Equity Coalition* to help bridge the gap in schools for marginalized and under-served communities by partnering with the school district to proactively meet these needs. She is the Director of Talent Management for *Internal Family Systems Institute* based in Chicago, IL. Her greatest success after the birth of her daughter is building a culture of learning, feedback and brave conversations and serving as a strategic business partner within the organizations she serves.

Contact Information

Email: Freedom@gdcarterpropertyinvestors.org

LinkedIn:

https://www.linkedin.com/in/donna-carter-a2201b15

Facebook: Donna Carter | Facebook

Be True To Your Unique Gifts

Franklin Fann

As a musician and music producer, I have over 30 years of recording experience and over 20 years of experience producing records. Additionally, I have written over 300 compositions, served in various churches as musical director in small churches as well as mega churches. I have worked with up-and-coming artists along with famous grammy award winners. I have travelled extensively throughout the United States in addition to extensive travel throughout Europe, Canada and Jamaica ministering the Gospel of Jesus Christ. I even had the privilege to minister in Rome, Italy at the Vatican before the late Pope John Paul. My experience and study of music has trained and equipped me to be a relevant and creative leader to help artists manifest their dreams and achieve their goals.

Traveling around the world and seeing the current trends in the music industry, I feel creative leadership is needed now more than ever before. It seems as if everyone is beginning to sound the same and even look the same. There are many artists who simply mimic the sound of other artists and many artists who are led astray from their true musical identity by leaders who lack creativity. This is a tremendous disservice to the artist, the general public and music connoisseurs like me. I believe artists in the music industries need creative leaders such as writers and producers who can help lead and guide them to identify their uniqueness and embrace what sets them apart from all of the other artists. This is a huge part of my purpose in life according to the plan God has destined for me. I want to help write and produce music that translates the unique distinctive sound of an artist and doesn't sound like every other song. I want to write and produce music that has meaning and fulfills the purpose of the artist's original intent.

Proverbs 3:27 says, *Do not withhold good from those who deserve it when it's in your power to help them* (NLT).

It is a blessing to be able to bless others, and God has graced me with the ability and opportunity to help others through music production. I don't take it lightly that God has given me the talent and ability to produce good music. I must acknowledge the source of my ability whenever the opportunity arises, and my source is God. He has blessed me as the founder and CEO of *BF Sounds Music Production Company,* where I help artists with writing and producing unique and distinct songs and albums. As a creative leader, I rely on the guidance of the Holy Spirit so I can provide sound advice based on the knowledge given to me by God and my experience.

1 Corinthians 12:7-8 says, *A spiritual gift is given to each of us so we can help each other. To one person the Spirit gives the ability to give wise advice; to another the same Spirit gives a message of special knowledge* (NLT).

This scripture is the basis of my approach to music production. I ensure every artist I work with is aware of the fact that I am not the lead or sole authority on their project. I am simply there to guide and provide wise advice based on the knowledge given to me by God. As a leader, I believe creative leaders should lead through guidance and not dictatorship. I don't want artists to feel as if they have no voice or no opinion in the production of their song. Ultimately, this is the key for me. It is "their" song, not mine. It is their vision and purpose for the song's creation, not mine. My task is to help artists find and develop their own sound.

Whatever their purpose and vision for bringing the song to me, I simply want to help them reach their goal and make their vision a reality. I don't want anyone to mimic me or my sound, so it is very important to me that the artist understands that I want them to be able to create a sound that comes from their heart and soul. A good leader allows their followers to evolve into their true self and not take on the whole persona of the leader. Although they may develop similar characteristics as the leader, they should still possess a major portion of their own identity. One must have a creative mindset to do this successfully.

As a matter of fact, before I meet with an artist, I pray and ask for Godly wisdom. I seek Him for guidance to specifically help each artist's music evolve throughout the time of production. Even during the production process, I am consistently seeking God for direction and guidance so I am able to give wise advice as necessary changes are made to get the desired result. I do not rely on or lean onto my own understanding, but I acknowledge the One who grants wisdom and knowledge to help me help others.

For instance, I am not necessarily a baker, but I approach music production like baking a cake. Baking a cake requires certain ingredients, and you must possess the right equipment and environment if you want a good cake. In addition to having the right ingredients, equipment, and environment, you also need knowledge and understanding to mix the ingredients and knowledge of proper usage of the equipment. Furthermore, you also need a little patience to wait for the finished product, and you need to trust that the hard work you put in will produce a great-tasting cake. I find that the patience part can sometimes be the most challenging part. In today's culture, instant gratification and quick satisfaction seem to be the norm. However, if you want a good and tasty cake, you must have some patience, and you must trust that the final result will be as you imagined, if not better than you imagined. Trust and believe; you do not want to eat an unfinished cake that was taken out of the oven prematurely.

Similarly, I take this same approach when I meet with an artist to determine the course of action in developing their song. I help them determine the right ingredients, the melody, harmony, rhythm, lyrics and song structure. I ensure we have the right equipment, such as microphones, singers, production equipment and musical instruments. Then I ensure we have an environment conducive to music making, my studio or a remote location. When the equipment and environment are determined and the right ingredients have been determined, and the recording has been completed, I now have to mix the ingredients for the song or the album. Next comes the hardest part of the production process, the patience and trust aspect.

I have found that many artists want instant success and gratification. This can be very challenging for me because, as I stated before, I am consistently praying and seeking God for direction. I am also trying to mix the ingredients appropriately to get the best sound imaginable. All of this takes time, and there have been occasions when the artist became impatient and lost trust during the process.

This can be very frustrating for the creative leader because you are forced to rush and possibly sign off on a project before you feel it is ready. Even in these moments, we have to realize that the artist is still the controlling factor, and we have to allow them the liberty to make the final decisions even when we disagree with them. This, too, is a part of the creative process in music production, allowing the artists to be free to choose and disagree with you. As a leader, this may seem like disobedience or rebellion, but we must learn that we can never force anyone to do anything.

Life is choice driven, and as creative leaders, we must allow people to make their own choices without pressure or force. Remember, we can only give wise advice and allow people to make decisions for themselves. Once they make the final decisions, they are accountable for the consequences of their decisions.

Creative leaders need to ensure that their followers are aware of the consequences associated with their decisions.

Pastor Franklin "Bubby "Fann, Jr.

Pastor Franklin "Bubby "Fann, Jr., is a husband, father, worshipper, music producer, songwriter, and world-renowned gospel recording artist. He serves as Lead Pastor and Chairman of the Board of Directors of "The Giver's Place "church. He is the only son of the late Bishop Franklin Fann, Sr., the late Mother Janet B. Fann, and has three sisters. His "Leading Lady" is his wife, Trisha Teenay Fann. He and his wife share countless family moments with their son Gary and grandson Elijah.

From the very womb of his Mother, Janet B. Fann, he was given back to the Lord for the service of ministry. He accepted The Lord Jesus and was filled with the Holy Spirit as a young man, and throughout his adult life was nurtured in holiness at his family church. From that nurturing, Pastor Bubby followed in the footsteps of his late father, Legacy Founder of The Giver's Place Church, and late grandfather, Bishop Willie C. Fann, as he answered the strong yearning and call of God to preach the Gospel.

Pastor Bubby became a licensed Minister of the Gospel in 2006 under the tutelage of Pastor Claybon Bogan at First Baptist Church of Jericho in Deptford, NJ. He served faithfully as Minister of Music there for many years and developed a hunger for the Word of God. He enrolled in the Bethany Baptist Association School of Biblical Studies and, in 2009, received his Ordination. From 2010 to 2012, Pastor Bubby sat under the leadership of Apostle Thomas Wesley Weeks at the New Destiny Fellowship Church in Wilmington, DE. In 2012, the Lord called him to serve at Glory Tabernacle Church, Bridgeton, NJ, under the leadership of his spiritual father, Bishop David A. Hadley, Sr. Pastor Bubby was appointed as Minister of Music and Youth Pastor and has faithfully served. In 2017 the Holy Spirit wrote the name "The Giver's Place" in his heart, and in 2020 founded, along with his wife, Leading Lady Trisha Teenay Fann, "The Giver's Place" church.

Now, their purpose is to steer the vision and mission of The Giver's Place" church with clarity and direction from God. They also vow to intentionally be imitators and followers of God, as instructed in Ephesians 5:1. The Fanns truly believe that, at "The Giver's Place," EVERY PERSON MATTERS!

Contact Information:

Facebook @Bubby.Fann

Instagram @BubbyFannLive

YouTube @Bubby Fann

Leadership Reimagined

Erika R. Erkard

Strong and effective leadership, in my opinion, always embodied two things primarily, consistency and success. Successful leaders are resilient, innovative, decisive, progressive, and constantly evolving, consistently achieving their goals while developing teams that would do the same. Their endgame is ultimately to stay in the leadership arena while being as effective as possible for as long as possible.

For years I thought this scenario encapsulated what a true leader should be, and I modeled my own leadership style accordingly. This picture-perfect view of leadership worked beautifully for me until life happened. A complex series of events that affected my family in stages over the last few years served to effectively reconstruct both my professional and personal life, and I wasn't ready for what resulted.

The leadership qualities I once utilized in business seemed to slip away from me exactly when I needed them most. Right in the middle of the unrelenting and catastrophic storms that engulfed me, every formula to win, every blueprint to overcome, every strategy to prevail failed me. Instead of being consistently successful, my life became a recurring series of inconsistencies and what I considered to be appalling failures. Despite my best efforts to rise above what seemed like insurmountable circumstances, each day presented a new set of challenges that ultimately gutted me mentally, physically, and emotionally.

The will to win, the drive to succeed, and the fortitude to persevere simply evaporated. And just like that, I was no longer a consistent and successful leader. In fact, I no longer had a clear and precise definition of what a leader should be. How could the label "leader" be attached to anything connected to me when failure seemed to be the only definitive and consistent component in my life?

I had never been in a darker and more desolate place than when I resigned from my job, cleared my ministry calendar, and stopped answering personal emails and phone calls. I had nothing to give, no clear timetable as to when this storm would subside and no options that would allow life to proceed as it once was. This new place was unfamiliar, uncomfortable, and disappointing.

In retrospect, the image of strong, decisive leadership I once held so dear faded with each passing day, and I must admit, I lost the strength to try and retrieve it. This was the story of a leader in freefall. I was tired, frustrated, angry at times and terrified that life might not offer a suitable reprieve which would allow me to recover from this experience quickly. "What happened to me?". is the question I pose to myself almost daily. Will I ever be an effective leader again? This is what could be considered the underbelly of leadership, the traumatic and unforeseen realities that refuse to be redirected by preplanned schedules, agendas, timetables, projections, or contracts.

How would I escape this leadership quagmire and recoup both my professional reputation and self-esteem? Was there a return from this barren wasteland of leadership inertia? Would I fully recover and regain the excitement and passion that once fueled me as a visionary and effective leader? These are some of the pressing uncertainties that have caused me to lie awake many nights, deprived of much-needed rest. To be perfectly transparent, the answers to those questions are still in flux, some being crystal clear and simple to capitalize on, while others remain unsettled and increasingly difficult to pin down.

After much painful soul searching, the realization that this season, representing a defining life moment, for me has become all too obvious. Though I've made difficult decisions to walk away from coveted projects and activities I enjoyed pursuing in a leadership capacity, I must make an important confession. I am now the person I always struggled to understand and, much to my shame, often judged harshly as a manager. That's my ugly personal truth.

I am now living the life of former colleagues and team members that I had very little tolerance for when they were struggling to remain relevant as leaders amid the effects of personal chaos they could neither fully explain nor escape.

Now leadership must exhibit professional compassion (if there is such a term) in addressing the professional aftermath of the employee's personal quandary. They must ask complicated questions that are both relevant and inevitable:

How does a team leader effectively engage someone who no longer functions at 100% capacity?

Should a responsible leader continue to provide growth opportunities for someone who is no longer consistent, or able to perform at their former capacity?

How does a manager/leader help the employee find a suitable means of valid contribution?

Can the company or team remain strong while supporting the individual who has become the weakest link?

When does the push to resume former output capacities give way to the acceptance of a new truth for both leader and team member?

How does a leader effectively determine when recovery is no longer an attainable goal?

How does the leader effectively manage the team member from a vantage point that utilizes their skills at a diminished performance level?

Will this adjustment negatively affect the team?

In these scenarios, what are the proper actions to take for everyone involved?

Lastly and perhaps most importantly, how are these questions filtered when they apply not to a team member or colleague but to yourself as a leader?

So many complex questions with so many potentially inconclusive outcomes.

My personal truth is I haven't always considered these questions where others were concerned, but now they are inescapable for me. My own personal life/leadership storm is giving me fresh insight that I hope will enlighten other leaders as well.

I've concluded that the feasible resolutions of these leadership conundrums can't be relegated to cookie-cutter approaches. This is not to say that leaders must readily embrace sub-par employee performance, but wouldn't it be wonderful if we could reach a place of empathetic consideration?

This would give both leaders and team members the opportunity to meet at tables of discussion to ascertain the best methods of progress for all parties concerned. A competent leader will always explore innovative ways to construct strong teams, even if that necessitates reconfiguring positions and job responsibilities, while conscientious team members will practice diligence in assessing what they can reasonably contribute to the overall health and stability of the team.

As a leader (and human being), I'm in recovery mode. I'm actively doing the work to discover where my new fit is and how that correlates to what I can successfully accomplish in this new place.

Again, my desire is not to be insensitive to the dynamics of individuality by suggesting a cookie-cutter approach to this scenario, but here are a few steps I'm taking to regain my leadership equilibrium:

Reaching out to my Higher Power

My Higher Power is God, and I'm trusting Him to walk me safely through this healing and recovery process. During the onslaught of this life storm, I've had some uncomfortably intrusive thoughts that led me to re-examine my spiritual health. Am I being punished? Have I done something wrong? Is God angry with me? These questions have pressed me to remember what His thoughts and plans are towards me.

"For I know the thoughts that I think toward you, saith the Lord, thoughts of peace, and not of evil, to give you an expected end." - Jeremiah 29:11

This passage of scripture assures me that I can fully trust God in this recovery process. His ultimate plan is to bring me to a place of success that encompasses the totality of my life, including but not limited to my leadership potential. Knowing this restores my confidence in every aspect of who I am, including the leadership skills I've been gifted with.

I've had to accept reality

For me this means resting in the fact that I'm doing the best I can now, and although my leadership skills are fully intact, their realistic functioning capacity has undergone a seismic shift. That's undeniably a dreadfully hard pill to swallow, but I'm embracing this realization in bite-size portions and benefitting greatly from ingesting absolute truth. Consistently reminding myself that I am still an effective leader both encourages and empowers me.

The valid choices I've made to care for my family and be fully present for them at this time reflect my continued ability to make sound leadership decisions. Doing what is best for myself and them means reassessing what is needed daily and moving accordingly. I'm not adjusting to this process perfectly, but each day is becoming easier to navigate.

Realize I haven't stopped moving forward

For quite a while, I struggled to grasp the fact that slowing to a pace I wasn't familiar with didn't equate to no longer being productive. I was accustomed to setting goals and accomplishing them at will. Suddenly, everything changed without warning, and I became afraid to continue pursuing my dreams.

Gradually the realization set in that this new and considerably measured stride was necessary for me to both regain and conserve my strength. Erroneously I once assumed the inability to systematically flow at 100% of my productivity capacity reflected failure and inconsistency, which is the exact opposite of what I have always strived to achieve.

Now I see the red flag flaws in my perceptions. In this present life storm, I've learned to prioritize what needs to be done and to do those things unapologetically. I can no longer function at 100%, at least not for the moment, but I am functioning at the speed and capacity that is healthy and best for me. I can do some things, and that is my new reality as a leader.

The outcome of this very complex journey is still unfolding before me. My family is still in a very serious storm, and I am braving the winds of that tempest with them. We are being changed collectively in the process and discovering that we are so much stronger when we stand and fight together.

Despite the personal challenges I face, familial responsibilities require me to function both as a team member and a leader. The landscape of leadership (for me) has changed to an almost unrecognizable terrain, yet I'm conquering my fears and regaining my leadership territory with each forward movement. I never imagined this type of challenge assaulting my life, but now I've had to reimagine leadership. In the process, I'm learning that leaders can recover from traumatic life circumstances in the very same manner as the team members they lead, consistently, successfully and one step at a time.

Erika R. Erkard

Erika and her husband, Thomas, have been married for 17 years and live in New Haven, CT. She is a family caregiver of 10+ years and has a great passion for supporting families who are navigating this often challenging and complicated process. In addition to teaching preschool and being a published author, she is the visionary of *Treasures in Earthen Vessels,* an online mentorship support platform, and the host of *Strength for the Journey,* an encouragement and support ministry program. Erika is currently pursuing a degree in Sociology and looking forward to expanding her leadership skills as a philanthropist and advocate for caregivers.

Feel free to reach her at tievgroup@yahoo.com or

https://www.facebook.com/erika.andersonerkard

Leadership or Ego-ship?

Elaine Sanders-Mayfield

Here's the thing, I'm not sure if my upper management promoted me into a leadership role because they thought I would be a good leader or because promotion was the reward for doing a great job. However, here's my take, I took that management position and ran with it! I decided to be the type of leader that celebrated their employees. I have experienced some wonderful leaders over the course of my 34-year career that were promoted for their brilliance, their performance and their ability to take the corporation to the next level coupled with excellent people skills. Those were the leaders I chose to emulate.

I would randomly send out an email and ask the team if they were interested in lunch. Many times, they brought their own lunch. A part of my growing pains was to learn to ask in advance. So, I would get an employee that I felt needed to feel more a part of the team send an email out stating that I would treat to lunch on a Friday. Who was interested? What did they have a desire for? I would have Italian, Chinese and hoagies delivered. My team was shocked to learn that I was not using my corporate card but my own personal money to show how much I appreciated them. I was an advocate of outdoor staff meetings changing the environment. I thought nothing of doing a Rita Water Ice run just to break up a busy summer day.

Being a creative, I always wanted to generate joy and stimulate a stale or boring work environment. Although I'm stern, I believe in developing specific boundaries, so that my employees know we can work smartly and play as well. I always reminded my team of the exorbitant amount of time spent in the workplace. We might as well make it worthwhile and fun doing what we do. My goal was to ensure my employees pulled into the parking lot excited to hit the ground running and energized to bring ideas. If they felt nervous pulling into the workplace parking lot, then I was not doing my job as a great leader. As a leader, you are not always able to celebrate your team with monetary rewards or promotions.

Aside from the standard or expected rewards, I celebrated them with certificates, lunch chits, Dunkin Donut gift cards for achieving a goal or resolving an issue. I practiced presenting these awards in front of their peers. When I attended leadership staff meetings, I included expressions of my team appreciation, who the awardees were and why they received the recognition. At that moment, I was trying to motivate other leaders to do the same.

A great leader recognizes their team members are people, not a commodity. I enjoyed hearing about the weekend and learning what sports their children played. It's important to understand what is truly of interest to your employees. Work, which is sometimes considered a bad word, is how we provide for our families and support our lifestyles. Work is not what we want to do; it's what we must do to survive in society.

So, with that in mind, I try to take the sting out of the words "have to work" and emphasize the humanistic side of what working affords us to do, such as activities with our families, taking vacations, attending sporting events, paying college tuition, buying a home, getting married all the things that create memories. The flip side is these items our jobs afford us are also stress points, i.e., college tuition payments and mortgages. Is this an easy task? No! However, a great leader won't stop until they figure it out.

I promised myself if I ever was in a leadership role that, I would serve my team as best as I could. What does that mean, Serve? I purposed to approach my leadership roles with the intent to understand the strengths and areas of improvement of each employee. Drive them to operate in their strengths while identifying areas that need strengthening. A strong leader will not use an employee's weaknesses to hold them hostage. The leader's goal is to drive excellence and motivate employees to be better versions of themselves. I get a thrill when employees feel safe to share with me how they intend to work on a weakness. What gives me that warm feeling is the fact that the employees felt safe sharing their plan with me. So how is this serving?

It's a form of serving because my mantra has always been to develop someone to take my position as the lead. A great leader is not intimidated by their employees. Exceptional team performance reflects good leadership. I am serving my team by giving credit where credit is due, not just behind closed doors but in team settings and upper management meetings above my level. Better yet, I would take an employee with me to an upper-management meeting for visibility. I enjoy serving my team by implementing their ideas which become a part of the daily practices.

The most important way I love to serve my team is to meet with each employee weekly; for more senior employees, we meet monthly. In the meetings, we review performance metrics. Metrics can be very cut and dry. In reviewing metrics, you can't ascertain the real muscle the employees exercised to achieve or accomplish tasks. So, while I encourage my employees to create a "Kudos Folder" of emails from customers or co-workers, colleagues saying thank you, I also have a "Kudos Folder" full of wonderful messages from colleagues, customers, and suppliers expressing the stupendous job performed by the employee.

I relished changing the narrative that leaders only keep track of an employee's mistakes or errors. Keeping track of the employees' successes and accomplishments makes it easier for a good leader to have a discussion pertaining to a skill set needing to be strengthened. A Kudos Folder not only highlights an employee's positive achievements, but it is a perfect segway to having that challenging discussion. But because the leader has changed the narrative and expressed the positive attributes of the employees, the employee wants to discuss how they can improve and in what areas.

You are probably thinking this sounds very unrealistic and like a fairy tale, but that's because there are some key attributes a great leader must display. Are you trustworthy? Can your employees trust you, the person, and trust you with information? While telling you, the employer, information that is freeing to the employee, how you process it and handle it determines the next level of trust with your employee.

An employee needs to be able to convey or express themselves to their employer without feeling judged, measured, or humiliated. And while the employee is being vulnerable and open with their leader, the leader must listen, be engaged, receptive, judgeless, and grateful.

A great leader's agenda is selfless, not selfish. The leader's motive should be how I can encourage, motivate, and optimize this employee's skills. When the agenda is selfless, the employer's personal motives (shining among peers, promotional opportunities) are lost. People feel protected, and integrity is mutual and respected by both employee and leader. When the agenda is selfless, the employees shine, and the employer finds joy in the employee shining.

This selfless approach is devoid of ego. We all have egos and exercising selflessness with the mission being to energize the team, build skillsets, and achieve goals is the ultimate assignment. When the focus is on the team and promoting them and providing visibility to them, leaders receive the visibility they aspire to organically.

Aspiring to be a great leader, I never felt like I arrived. Even if I achieved awards for leadership and received accolades from my team, I'm always thinking about how I can do more. Many have heard the comment that if a teacher has a class that the majority are failing, then there is an issue with the teacher. If one student is failing, then the student needs help. A great leader is interested in the success of all their employees based on their capabilities. There will be found among your employees some leaders, some "steady eddies" and what I call sleepers; they don't know what they want to be, however; they start to bloom and finally see a career path.

The last thought I want to share is that a good leader listens intently! Not only does a great leader listen to the ideas, thoughts and suggestions of employees, but they give the ideas life and legs, and they become integrated into the business. I mentioned this earlier, and here is the other side of listening.

One of my best employees was Amy Kroll, smart and brilliant. I loved that she was outspoken, and came to me. She asked to have a moment. I'm an advocate of stopping what I'm doing if someone comes to me with concern. Amy expressed I always looked well put together, and while I shared stories of my career to relate to my employees, I never told them my horror stories. I seemed too perfect. I appeared as if I had this perfect stellar career. I listened and did not react or retaliate because, oh boy, did I have horror stories.

In my next staff meeting, we reviewed metrics and aged items. I always thought I was transparent and gave helpful information to help them resolve issues. However, after my discussion with Amy, some self-reflection, and gathering true life examples, I began to share in my meeting. I started out with, "This issue reminds me of when I royally screwed up." Their eyes lit up! Now there is a balance, too many horror stories – you appear incompetent. Pace yourself.

Every now and then, drop a nugget or horror story of how you made a mistake, how you fixed it and how you are open to helping resolve issues. My favorite saying was, "There is nothing we can't fix!" My vulnerability and openness made me touchable, relatable, and human to my team. I am ever so grateful to Amy for her candidness, honesty, and bravery in telling me about myself. Most employees would let it go, but she felt I cared and wanted me to be better because I invested in them being better.

At the end of the day, my best days were when I could make my employees smile, feel acknowledged, valued, and empowered. I trust and believe God that I am not an anomaly.

Elaine Sanders-Mayfield

Elaine Sanders-Mayfield retired after 34 years from one of the largest defence companies in the world. Elaine's years of experience included leadership roles in Supplier Diversity, Compliance as a Business Area Lead and Procurement Management. Elaine started in an entry-level position and continued to move up the corporate ladder with assignments of increased responsibilities.

Elaine is taking advantage of her retirement, pursuing her passion in singing Gospel music and spreading the Good News. She has released an EP "K. Elaine" (2012), CD entitled "*Simply Elaine*" (2016) and most recently released a single, "*While I Wait*". In addition to ministering in song, Elaine provides mentoring, coaching, resume creation/update and mock interviews to career-oriented individuals.

Elaine shares her success and passions with her supportive husband of almost 20 years, Thomas A. Mayfield.

Contact Information

Karmelthomas64@comcast.net

Karmelelaine@gmail.com

10 Essential Attributes of Great Creative Leadership

Pastor Job Daniel Chintakayala

As a Creative Leader and Pastor, there's always a list of things to 'do.' Every week I find myself in a series of meetings, all with outcomes and agenda items. If I'm not careful, I can begin to think that leadership is simply about getting things done. It begs the question. Am I just the leader, or am I actually leading?

You may have a title or position of leader, but are you leading your team? Are you functioning as the leader? The reality is leadership is about people. It's not just about getting things done. Our role is to take the people we are responsible for leading from where they are now to where God would have them be.

Leadership doesn't just happen. It's something we need to actively think about, pursue, and develop.

Recently I read about a study in INC. magazine by the management consulting firm Zenger Folkman on the attributes of great leaders. They ranked leadership skills most important for success by interviewing over 330,000 bosses and employees, asking about the traits that great leaders have. The results were interesting to me because they don't just apply to corporate leaders but, in fact, to all leaders, especially creative leaders within a Church context.

I wonder as you read the following which you need to develop or continue to develop in your own leadership?

So here are the top 10 traits that we, as creative leaders, can focus on developing for maximum success.

1. Great Leaders are able to inspire and motivate other people.

Inspiring other people will come naturally to some but not to most. For most of us, it's something we will need to work on in order to become the creative leader we're called to be. If you're wondering why you're having trouble getting your team to do what you need them to do, perhaps it's because you're not inspiring them. Perhaps your communication is lacking, boring, or seemingly irrelevant.

Or are you giving them something to follow and something to be inspired by? Are you the sort of person that others want to follow?

Your level of enthusiasm and passion is rubbing off on them, for better or worse.

When you communicate with your team, do they respond with enthusiasm or apathy? If you're going to be a great creative leader, you need to learn the art of inspiring other people.

2. Great leaders have high levels of integrity and honesty.

Ephesians 4:1 encourages us to "live a life worthy of the calling." It's exhorting us to live weighty lives like a set of scales where the call of God is on one side, and our lives are on the other. Our lives are meant to measure up to the call.

When it comes to integrity and honesty, those in the business world see the value of these attributes in leadership. How much more in the Church should we value and possess these characteristics?

3. Great leaders solve problems and analyze issues.

It's easy to see problems and to point the finger at the person who caused the problem. In far too many organizations, this is the normal mode of operating. The Church should be different. We know that it's in unity that God brings blessing. So, when problems arise, let's be great leaders who approach problems differently. Let's look for solutions. Let's solve problems and create unity instead of pulling unity apart by finger-pointing and accusation.

4. Great leaders have a personal drive for results.

If you've been given the privilege of a leadership position and you don't have a drive for results, then I'd be questioning whether you're the right person to be in that position. I think about this regularly in my own life – where am I driving for results? What am I making happen? Am I waiting to be told, to be pushed, or am I the one on the front foot taking personal responsibility?

5. Great leaders communicate powerfully and prolifically.

As a leader, you will probably have to repeat yourself (a lot) in order to get your message across. Communicating your message powerfully doesn't mean being abrasive or aggressive, but it does mean creating an impact. Great leaders know this, and they don't become tired of their own voice either. Instead, they know that people often need to hear the message many times and in many different ways to actually take it in. The message may stay the same, but the method can and should change. Either way, though, know that in order to be a great creative leader, you will need to grow your tenacity and ability to communicate powerfully, over and over again. It's through this communication that you will build culture, create a common vision, and lead your team effectively.

6. Great leaders build authentic relationships.

Some leaders choose to remain distant from the people they lead. They pretend to have a relationship, but the reality is they don't. People can tell if you genuinely care for them or not. If you use people simply to get your thing achieved, eventually, they will realize that you don't care for them like they thought you did. It will hurt them, you, and things will end up going backwards.

Great leaders realize they can't know everyone, but they can know some people, and they choose to build authentic relationships with these people. They don't use people to get stuff done. Instead, they build meaningful, real, intentional and authentic relationships. Then they partner with those people to achieve the vision together.

7. Great leaders display professional and technical expertise.

I'm sure we all want our teams to be excellent. We want them to be the very best they can be. We expect this of them. But do we have the same expectations of ourselves? Are we leading in the area of expertise? Great leaders don't settle or become stagnant in their expertise.

They say it takes 10,000 hours to become an expert. The truth is those hours have to be intentional. We can't just pass the time and think our expertise is getting any better. Instead, we need to proactively work on our expertise (leadership, pastoring, communication, shepherding, people skills etc.) if we're going to be great creative leaders.

8. Great leaders create strategic perspectives.

Great leaders don't just have a vision or know the vision; they create strategies for achieving the vision. In the context of Hillsong Creative, we don't have our own departmental vision; we own Pastor Brian's vision for our church. But knowing what the vision is and achieving that vision are completely different things. A great leader knows the vision and works on a plan to make it happen.

9. Great leaders develop others.

People don't always come "readymade." It's not often that someone will walk into your life or team and solve all of your problems. Instead, people come willing, and then it's up to us to develop in them the attributes they need to contribute meaningfully. Often this will take a lot of time and intentionality. Great leaders don't look past the person who isn't ready yet, they see the potential in them, and they commit to the journey of developing them.

10. Great leaders Innovate.

When you do what you do week in and week out, it's easy to stay within the safety and rhythm of the known. Great leaders don't just play it safe, though. In order to grow others, to lead others, and to go beyond the average, great creative leaders push forward with new ideas and new ways of doing things.

The Bible depicts God in this way. He is often "doing a new thing", but at the same time, He doesn't abandon the good of the present. To be great leaders, we need to emulate Him. Looking for and creating the news without throwing out the good things He's already built. Often the present can be a foundation for the future. A great leader will learn from the past, be grateful for the blessing of the present, but also keep passionately pursuing innovation to take us into the future.

Let's be intentional about leading and growing in our leadership as we do all we can to be the creative leaders we're called to be.

Blessings,

Pastor Job Daniel, India

Job Daniel Chintakayala

Job Daniel Chintakayala graduated from Maranatha Bible College. He was a Pastor in India for the last 18 years doing ministry among the tribes, reaching the unreached lost, perishing souls for Christ Ministry among leprosy people, Bonda tribe people helping the poor in tribal villages during the Corona crisis.He lives in the Visakhapatnam Andhra Pradesh state, south India with his wife, Shanthi Job, and his two children, David and Nissy.

Pastor Job Daniel Chintakayala is the founder and the president of *"Word of Hope Interior Ministries International"* serving as senior pastor for the *Word of Hope Interior* church in Visakhapatnam City and involved in teaching and preaching the gospel across India.

Contact Info

Cell/whatsapp+919000943154.

E-mail: job12daniel@gmail.com.

Facebook: Job Daniel Chintakayala

Creative Leadership: A Recipe For Success

Lydia Ford

Ladies and gentlemen, when I saw Yvette post the "Creatives" topic, I was excited about the opportunity to make my contribution to this anthology, and at the same time, feeling overwhelmed with my current workload. But nevertheless, I decided to give it a shot.

After giving some thought to how to approach the topic, "The Creatives," a thought came to my mind. I began to think about all the preparation, ingredients, process and time I put into making my famous 5 Flavor Pound Cake. You see, you must start with the basics, the equipment, the ingredients, utensils, measuring tools, an area to do the baking and the energy mode to complete the process.

A creative leader is someone with a lot of energy, and a vision, a plan or path to seeing it come to fruition. From the time I was a little girl, I always saw my mom making pound cakes in the kitchen. I watched her make it from start to finish. I looked at everything she had set aside to make the pound cake. Mom told me that you should never start making a pound cake before 10 o'clock in the morning; make sure you preheat the oven, set the eggs, and butter out the night before and use cake flour for the best results. She specifically told me that I had to have the right frame of mind in order for the cake to turn out right. My mom bakes her cake for an hour and twenty minutes, give or take a few minutes. The true test for checking to see if it's done is to stick a toothpick in the center. If it comes out dry, the cake is done. When I was a child, my siblings and I always got to lick the spatula and take our fingers and run them around the bowl to get a taste of the remaining cake batter.

Making a pound cake from scratch, like leadership takes skill, preparation, timing, passion, creativity, a positive mindset, confidence, and problem-solving skills. When I became an adult, I tried unsuccessfully on numerous occasions to make the Fulton Pound Cake. I even gave up one time and decided to focus on making sweet potato and apple pies instead. But one day, I decided that pound cakes were a part of my heritage, and I wasn't going to stop until I became proficient at it.

Creative Leadership takes persistence, motivation, and determination. Failure is not an option! It takes passion and belief in what you are trying to achieve. At last, I reached my goal. I did so well that I began to improvise and experiment with different combinations of the five spices my mom normally used. I decided to add a 6th spice on occasion, and to my surprise, the pound cake smelled and tasted exceptionally flavorful.

Creative leaders are not afraid to try new things. They are innovators, pioneers, and they color outside the lines. They also inspire and encourage their team to think independently and intuitively so that they can grow and be exceptional in their own right.

A few years ago, I began advertising and selling my five flavored pound cakes on my website and Facebook page. Word of mouth spread, and soon I had my own "Lydia For Sensational Salads and Pound Cakes" business cards and Facebook Ads.

Leadership requires business acumen, training, self-discipline, and decision-making. A good businessperson must investigate whether there is a market for their ideas. You must weigh the pros and cons and make sure you have a great business plan. This is an area where most of us novices need expert advice. So, my advice to you is to invest in someone who can assist you with technology, marketing, and production.

In the beginning, I had to figure out why my cake kept falling, why it wasn't moist on the inside, and determine how long to cook it in my own oven. I had to ask Mom some questions like, "What kind of flour do you use? How many eggs to put in? How long do you mix the batter?" etc. A great leader must follow the strategies and patterns of experts that have garnered success in their enterprise. Only after you've mastered the technique should you make a move to employ your own standard and style before you unleash your own brand or creativity.

Creative leaders are not born with a silver spoon in their mouths. I don't believe everyone is born to be a leader. I do believe leadership can be taught and learned, but you must have passion, driving strategies and skills to become successful. It takes imagination, original ideas, and artistic combination to produce a product that becomes sought after by the public.

Although I longed to make the "Fulton Pound Cake," the fact that my last name was Fulton did not mean I would automatically be able to replicate the famous Fulton Pound Cake. I had to be taught. I had to learn. It took time. And I had to be persistent and consistent in the midst of failing repeatedly.

Creative Leadership means that you must continue learning and not be afraid of coming up short or failing. As leaders, we must allow our mentees and our team to fail and encourage them to try again. Leaders are visionaries, strong communicators, and active listeners. Mentees must endure both positive and negative criticism.

Leaders must engage and help their team to envision the end product before it appears before their eyes. It's like faith, "The substance of things hoped for, the evidence of things not seen."

I had seen my mama's pound cake down through the years, but when I became an adult, I had the opportunity to envision what my own pound cake would look like.

Though I failed over and over again, I was determined to succeed. I became motivated to see what I could achieve by deciding to keep at it until I reached perfection. Great leaders motivate their team. My mom kept encouraging me to keep practicing. Creative Leaders are resilient; they keep getting knocked down, but never knocked out! I was confident that eventually, my cake would make it into the "Fulton Hall of Fame."

Creative Leadership looks like community, a commonplace, a sense of belonging to a group or a tribe where you fit in. My tribe consisted of my parents, siblings, grandparents and extended family and friends. The kitchen and dining room table were where family met, communicated, and experienced the aromas and festive meals mom cooked every day but especially on holidays.

Every leader is looking for their tribe. As the visionary or innovator, the creative leader's thirst and longing is to build a team that can share experiences both good and bad. They help their team grow and reach their full potential, produce relevant materials, develop powerful stories and create lasting relationships. Leaving a legacy of success, excellence, resilience, determination, and servanthood to the next generation is important to me.

Confident leaders, coaches and mentors are those who lead the team. They pour in wisdom and make sure the team members learn and develop the qualities of leadership. I learned a lot about being a leader by observing my mother, grandmother and aunties who were leaders that served in the church. I learned about hospitality and serving by sitting in the kitchen and listening to stories at the feet of my elders.

Creative leaders model and that affords the team to learn "Best Practices" from the role models in their family to renowned leaders like John Maxwell, Steve Jobs, Oprah Winfrey etc. It is the leader's job to oversee and bring the team into the metamorphosis that becomes the team's crowning achievement. Once the process is complete, you're left with a masterpiece, a work of art, or a life that will forever be changed as a direct result of your impact upon them.

Creative leadership celebrates when a collective, as well as a personal goal, is achieved. Helping others discover their passion and purpose is a big turn-on for me. Through my tenure in Women's Ministry, my pastoral ministry, *Early Morning Tea*, and *Building Fruitful Friendships* brands, I've had opportunities to partner with other ministries, to train and equip women to operate in positions and roles in my ministry and in my entrepreneurial activities.

I've also been on the opposite side as a learner and mentee of Min. Sharon J. Savage, my mentor. She afforded me the opportunity to learn from her. She is a global leader, an international preacher, teacher, evangelist, and mission's coordinator. Through this relationship, I was able to experience traveling internationally to Kimana, Kenya to minister, teach and train a group of widows for an entire week. That opportunity gave me the tools to identify leaders among the group of women who had the desire and passion to start a women's widow support group in their community.

A great leader is also a good listener. When I went to Kenya, I developed my own teaching curriculum on the topic I was given. My topic was: Widows Rising Up to Pursue Your Purpose. After the first few days, I realized that the material was good, but it was over their heads. Even though I had an interpreter, the women were not responding. My Mentor. Min. Sharon sat in my class those first couple of days. She told me that I needed to connect with the women, change my strategy and allow them the opportunity to talk about their lives as widows in Kenya.

Great leaders must be both creative and humble! You have to know when something is not working and not try to force your own way of thinking, or your own agenda down someone's throat. I decided to let the women speak to tell their own stories, and express their grief, misery and sorrow. It worked!! They opened up. It was refreshing; deliverance had taken place along with many tears. During the last two days, we role-played what a widow's support group might look like for them. I asked for volunteers to lead and participate in the mock meeting. One person volunteered to pray, someone agreed to read scripture, and another person led a song familiar to everyone. A woman named Helen agreed to facilitate the meeting. Out of that trial meeting, a leader was born. Helen Butaki became a leader that day. She took my teaching manual and started a widow's support group in her hometown of Katale, Kenya.I assisted by sending her teaching materials, books, and other supplies. I am her mentor and spiritual mother.

Mentoring individuals in ministry and in my business adventures invigorates me. I love seeing my mentees evolve and develop the gifts and skills they didn't realize they had. I've had the pleasure of leading women's ministry programs, creating teaching content, helping to facilitate prayer partnerships, creating a women's ministry newsletter, and conducting invigorating, spiritual women's programs and conferences during my years as pastor of *Don't Forget To Say Your Prayers International*. In conclusion, I'd like to add that sometimes grief and loss can affect leadership in unimaginable ways.

God often takes trauma, a chaotic situation, along with suffering and loss to create a brand-new tapestry of your life.God often takes your misery and turns it into a ministry with a message for you and me. A lot of times, God uses a messy situation and gives you a message. A lot of secular businesses and entrepreneurial as well as spiritual enterprises were born out of someone's misery or pain. Your suffering can be the impetus that births another component of your creative leadership style. The death of my daughter and husband in 2010 and 2011 catapulted me into becoming a first-time author. I used my writing skills to tell the story of my grief journey. I was blessed to become a first-time author. I used the language in my story to help individuals who have suffered a loss understand that it is okay to question God. And to be angry with Him, especially in areas related to unanswered prayers or prayers that were not favorable to our situation.

My creative style and brands have flowed from each transition point in my life. The Pandemic thrust me into online preaching and teaching. My desire to keep in touch with the masses and particularly women, led me to create a morning Devotional hour called *Early Morning Tea*. Tea is one of my favorite morning beverages, so with a great devotional book, I got started doing EMT at 8:00 Monday, Wednesday, and Friday. After a year, I decided to brand the concept and had one friend create a poster and another create a logo. I uploaded the logo to Vista Print, and they put it on a mug. I began marketing and selling my EMT mugs to my followers and friends. Each of these projects has been instrumental in creating my digital footprint on multiple social media platforms.

Most of the leadership positions I have had were derived that way or they evolved from a very dark time in my life. It often seems like I was born for adversity or born to help solve a problem or to help soothe the pain in someone's soul.

Over the years, I've discovered that people, women in particular, long for connection. Women are community oriented. They are looking for their tribe, their sister, girlfriend circle. In order to get women connected to other women, each woman has to know they are "Enough." Creative Leaders discern when a door of opportunity opens. When the eyes of your understanding are open to an incredible moment when you say to yourself, "I need to write this book, brand this concept, make it my own, create a logo or artistic work of art."

I often tell my mentees and viewers that opportunity isn't going to come and sit down next to you and cross its legs and wait on you to bust a move. Leadership opportunities like creating the Fulton 5 Favored Pound Cake take learning, teamwork, passion, time, effort, motivation, a positive mindset, perseverance, and creativity. Opportunity keeps moving. So, you had better run and catch up with it before it passes you by.

Rev. Lydia Ford

Lydia Ford is a licensed and ordained minister of the Gospel. She is the CEO of *Lydia Ford International Ministries*. She is a transformational leader that works across denominations and defies stereotypes and biases. The ministry exists to help develop and mature the body of Christ. It recognizes that all Kingdom work is not done within the confines of the church building. Rev. Ford is an internet digital creator. She hosts three groups on Facebook: *Early Morning Tea, Building Fruitful Friendships* and *Grace2Win*. She uses these social media platforms to instruct, encourage, influence, and equip her followers with skills and strategies to develop and improve their lives, create opportunities for mentorship, leadership development, encourage friendships and partnerships with other women.

Rev. Ford's passion is teaching and mentorship. She enjoys training and developing women so that they can grow in their faith, gifts, and purpose. She has a zeal to address the lack of an individual's basic resources needed to exist in a society where so many people are marginalized, hurt, and economically depressed. Rev. Ford is a published author. Her books recount the heartfelt feelings and emotions derived from her five-year journey of two life-changing events: The death of her daughter Danielle Ford-Geter and the death of her husband, Thomas Ford, in 2010 and 2011, respectively. She is devoted to helping people who are stuck in grief to get unstuck. As a grief counselor and CEO of *Grace2Win Counseling Services*, she equips individuals with skills and strategies that emphasize not just coping with grief but winning, thriving, and moving on in purpose after grief.

Contact Info
Grace2win720@gmail.com
www.thegrace2win.com

Education as the Practice of Creation, Reinvention, and Radical Dreaming: An Autobiographical Account of Teaching in the 21st Century

Chiara Mahogany White-Mink

"When I dare to be powerful, to use my strength in the service of my vision, then it becomes less and less important whether I'm afraid." –Audre Lorde

Teaching as the Intersection of the Personal and Political and as Social Justice Work

I come from a long cultural tradition of creation, reinvention, and radical dreaming. For centuries, the Black woman's elevated consciousness and unwavering commitment to freedom permanently altered spaces to which she was never invited or welcomed. Anna Julia Cooper — one of the most prominent African-American scholars in United States history — published *A Voice From The South* in 1892, a series of speeches that engendered the birth and evolution of Black feminism; Fannie Lou Hamer—a dynamic leader in the Black Freedom Struggle who was known for her work around voting rights and women's rights — coined the idiomatic phrase, "I'm sick and tired of being sick and tired" in a 1964 speech, a pithy critique of slow social progress, what the late Rev. Dr. Martin Luther King Jr. characterized as "... [creeping] at horse and buggy pace" (King, 1963); bell hooks — a writer, speaker and educator well-versed in intersectional feminism—-imagines an educational system that doesn't "bureaucratize the mind" (Freire, 1985) but functions as the practice of freedom in *Teaching to Transgress*, a collection of essays published in 1994; Alice Walker — the great American novelist and social activist — developed the term womanism to emphasize the uniqueness and complexity of the Black woman's experience; Audre Lorde — a melodic poet, speaker, and activist — confronted interlocking systems of oppression with an unmatched ferocity and complicated our understanding of power; and Megan Thee Stallion — a contemporary female rapper who is known for her confidence and unapologetic sensuality — invented the word "traumazine" to describe her journey grappling with painful life experiences. Admittedly, I associate creation, reinvention, and radical dreaming with Black women; and consequently, I conceptualize change-making and culture-shifting as an inherited responsibility. No one can convince me that our capacity to envision and reimagine is not our greatest asset.

Though most of the women I have named are respected for their contributions to academic and intellectual matters, I have watched Black women from various backgrounds engage in this sacred cultural work. I would argue that our interpretive frameworks — the set of experiences, social identities and belief systems that influence how we navigate the world — position us as paragons of activism and social change.

My commitment to creation, reinvention, and radical dreaming in the classroom is inextricably linked to my secondary educational experiences. Characterized by ontological, epistemological, and axiological rigidity, my experiences in secondary classrooms elicited resistance, which seemed to be a plausible response because I viewed those spaces as unjust. Eventually, resistance turned into shapeshifting and contorting because (a) I needed to survive and (b) I envisioned attending a 4-year university, and pacifying teachers seemed to be the way to go about this. I had reached a point where education and encroachment became synonymous, indistinguishable terms. In undergraduate school, I began to reflect on my experiences in secondary schools. I read books/articles from scholars such as Lisa Delpit, Paulo Friere, and Gloria Ladson-Billings. They helped me understand how social and systemic factors — such as race, gender, social class, etc. — contributed to my feelings of frustration and sometimes inadequacy in educational environments. All of this acquired wisdom led me to pursue a career in teaching. I vowed to approach teaching as social justice work so that I could support students in challenging convention and transforming the world.

Inside the Public School Classroom: Gloria Naylor's The Women of Brewster Place and Kwame Alexander's The Crossover.

Prior to receiving my first teaching assignment in Worcester (MA), I suspected that creation would be an essential component of my experience, particularly with regard to the curriculum. After all, I spent much of my time critiquing public education and researching alternate solutions in undergraduate school. I had come too far to succumb to the demands of an oppressive institution.

To hold myself accountable for the growth and development of my students and my practice, I drafted a disciplinary teaching philosophy that promoted the conscious coupling of critical literacy and disciplinary literacy (my English classes will ALWAYS be infused with history and sociology); the critical examination of student sense-making processes, which includes operating under the contention that students are always making sense (even when I don't understand what governs their thinking); and the preservation of the human spirit — that is, ensuring the holistic student is welcomed into my classroom and that the assets they bring are mined and leveraged. The needs of our nation's culturally and linguistically diverse student population are constantly changing, so it's a document I'm not afraid to revisit and adjust as necessary.

Under the tutelage of like-minded veteran educators, I developed two units that centered the humanity of my students. The first unit — *"Pass the Mic, America: Honoring the Humanity of Women of Color"* — explored why we read stories about women of color and how these stories shape our sense of reality, how these stories add to the national discourse on gendered racism, the conditions that influence their experiences, and how they exercise agency and get closer to freedom.

We read Gloria Naylor's *The Women of Brewster Place* (along with supplemental texts such as Rihanna's *S&M*) to aid us in this exploration. It is also worth mentioning that I had to pitch this text to my mentor teacher and my university mentor, order the books, and create my own classroom activities and projects since I was the first at the school to use this text. Every essential question and assignment was carefully constructed, and every supplementary text carefully chosen.

After we analyzed the text and completed the accompanying assignments, I was left with several thoughts. (1) Many of my students found sensitive ways to insert their truths, even if they were antithetical to popular opinions (this is important to note because many students have a difficult time disagreeing with each other in classroom discussions). For example, one of my young men of color felt the text conveyed the worst traits men (particularly Black men) could embody. He explained that the men in his life hold themselves to much higher standards.

Prior to this comment, students were solely fixated on the destructive behavior of the male characters. I respected his desire to show that men can and do overcome toxic masculinity despite its ubiquity and its historical role in perpetuating social inequities. Additionally, his decision to share his perspective and worldview reflected one of my core beliefs about classroom discussions: discussions should promote divergent thinking. Another student suggested that the men behaved so poorly because extremity leads to conspicuity. In other words, Naylor's construction of the Black male was necessary to draw attention to patriarchy as a pronounced and harmful system of injustice. (2) Solidarity on the basis of shared identity is never guaranteed. I assumed that my Black female students would resonate with the Black female characters. Contrary to my assumptions, they were not as empathetic to the African-American female characters. They acknowledged racist, sexist, and heteronormative societal expectations, but they also emphasized choice, agency, and hope as key ingredients for accessing freedom. (3) Teaching and learning occur simultaneously.

My students' commentary throughout the unit helped me understand the text in a way I had never understood it before. Though I had previously acknowledged the characters' resilience, student perspectives helped broaden my thinking considerably.

My new analysis of the text includes how resiliency functions throughout the text. Resiliency is possible because the characters cling to human connection as a means of survival. The human connection that matters most is the relationships black women possess with one another. I discovered this book is not about the toxic relationships women possess with men. It is about how the factors that dictate and govern the way we navigate our world teach us the intrinsic value and necessity of radical love, human connection, sisterhood, and community.

Gloria Naylor highlights pervasive social issues to help readers conceptualize the intensity, depth, and promise of human relations. (4) Students can and will form their own opinions when teachers guide them. As a Black woman, it would have been easy to suffocate students with my own beliefs and opinions about the experiences of women of color. Instead, I provided appropriate guiding questions and resources and allowed the students to embark on their own intellectual journey. Students were able to internalize the importance of inquisition, exploration, and collective learning, and they recognized the dangers of blind assertions and irresponsible engagement.

The second unit — *Beyond The Pod1: What "Non-Academic" Activities Teach Us About Ourselves, Each Other, and the World We Inhabit* — was inspired by Kwame Alexander's *The Crossover* and the film *Coach Carter*. Both texts fervently support the following notion: education extends beyond the confines of a classroom. Schools are indeed framed as a student's primary center of learning; however, the potential to learn also exists outside of the classroom.

With this unit, I encouraged students to bring their full selves to the classroom and connect with me, each other, the text, and the world, all while getting intimate with themselves. This unit made two things evident: (1) students, no matter how much they grumble, will meet high expectations, especially when rapport-building is prioritized, and (2) students are always learning whether or not they know it.

In their final project, each student was able to name at least five lessons they learned by participating in extracurricular activities, things they would likely not acquire in an academic setting. Similar to *The Women of Brewster Place* unit, I was the first at the school to use this text, so the ritualistic passing down of resources and lesson plans did not happen. And this was my first year of teaching!

Inside the Private School Classroom: Zora Neale Hurston's *Their Eyes Were Watching God* and Beyonce's *Lemonade*

Beyonce will always have a home in my curriculum; therefore, I welcome teaching in schools that grant curricular autonomy, like private schools. Using Beyonce's *"Pretty Hurts,"* my students were tasked with exploring how words work together to produce meaning. I chose this song because of its universal relevance (read:

---

[1] Pod refers to a set of classrooms in a specific area of the school. Each classroom was demarcated by makeshift walls.

an explicit critique of beauty standards), its accessibility, and its ability to complicate what we deem analysis worthy (*i.e.*, usually western canonical literature). I'm also interested in creating opportunities for my youth to engage with Black writers, poets, musicians, and thought-leaders in academic environments.

Modeled after the tasks in Nancy Dean's *Voice Lessons*, I created a low-stakes assignment that permitted students to become intimate with the language. Language is mesmerizing, romantic even. When you allow it to seduce you, to tease you, to envelop you, you'll develop a refined or newfound appreciation for it.

I've been in love with language since I was a child. It's the safest, most precious love affair I've known. Because my approach to teaching is more process-oriented, I'm interested in HOW my students make sense of language. I'm interested in their observations, their questions, their inferences, and their explorations. They need to show me — through a focused analysis of language—why their interpretations of the text are tenable.

My classroom is their intellectual playground. Quite frankly, knowledge of western canonical literature is advantageous; however, in order to curate a holistic experience for young people who are living in an increasingly multicultural and diverse world, we must deviate from the dead white folk sometimes. Additionally, we must adjust how we teach these texts (e.g. what frameworks we employ, what systems of knowledge govern our approach to teaching, etc.).

To date, one of my favorite units is the one I created centered on *Their Eyes Were Watching God (Eyes)* and *Lemonade* (what I jocularly refer to as "The Black Women Takeover"). While the pairing of these texts was not my idea, I do not know any other educators who have used these texts together; therefore, once again, I created every resource from scratch. This unit began with a close reading and rhetorical analysis of a song from the album (lyrics + music video), followed by a series of in-class presentations where students presented their findings and lingering questions. Each presentation helped students think about why I would teach these texts together, or in other words, how these texts conversed with each other.

After their presentations, students submitted a metacognitive think-write. They answered the following questions: (1) Describe your experience analyzing this body of work. How does your interpretive framework – comprising your lived experiences, social identities, and value systems (and, of course, their intersections) – influence the way you approached this text? You may want to begin by thinking about the relationship you formed to/with *Lemonade*. Was it purely cognitive/cerebral/academic/intellectual? Emotional? Spiritual? A combination of the three? Did you experience a sense of disconnect? Explore your relationship to the piece and explain the factors that shaped this relationship (don't forget to think about the historical context that undergirds your interpretive framework, as we don't exist in vacuums). Be honest and forthcoming.

Part of engaging with art produced by members of marginalized social groups is thinking about responsible consumption. (2) What did you learn? How has your thinking shifted over the course of the semester? How does this album illustrate the mantra, "When life gives you lemons, you make lemonade?" What does this album contribute to the national discourse on matters of race, gender, and language? (3)Talk to me about the overall experience of deviating from traditional English texts. How was the experience of analyzing a combination of lyrics, iconography, poetry (Warsan Shire's brilliance) and music? (4) Now that you've viewed other presentations, discuss potential connections between *Eyes* and *Lemonade*.

Remember, avoid [exclusively] thinking about literal and micro-level connections. Think of cultural, historical, linguistic, and sociopolitical connections. Many songs in the album contain religious/biblical references (to God). What function does God serve in how Beyonce chooses to interpret her life experiences, and what can we infer about God's presence in *Their Eyes Were Watching God? Who is God?* How might the characters engage with God throughout the text based on the title? Explain. (5) Is there anything else you want/need to share with me about this project, this album, or this class? What would you change/modify/adjust about the project (for example, if I were to do this again, I'd screen the entire visual album in class and keep the songs in chronological order).

Truthfully, I was apprehensive about this project. I was uncomfortable by the prospect of my predominantly white, upper-middle-class students analyzing Beyonce's metaphorical odyssey. I questioned whether they had the tools to approach her art critically and sensitively, and if they did not possess those skills, I wondered if I could muster up the energy to teach them (racial fatigue is real!).

As a Black woman who has a spiritual, emotional, psychological, and intellectual connection to *Lemonade*, protecting Beyonce's art was my duty, even if I was protecting it from school children without malevolent intentions. To my surprise, students responded well to this project. They presented high-quality analyses and adopted an inquisitive approach instead of a judgemental or accusatory one.

I find that questions (rather than statements or declarations) are easier to address. This project reminded me that students when given the opportunity, can find entry points or sources of connection no matter how different the author's experience seems. For instance, Lemonade addresses topics such as anger, accountability, and hope.

If students can reflect on times in their own lives where they have felt angry or hopeful, or accountable, they can form a relationship with the album. After reading the student feedback, I learned that this was one of their favorite projects of the year, and some of them even added songs from the album to their respective playlists. Most importantly, some students shared that their perspective on music shifted. They now viewed songs as analysis-worthy texts. I would say this was a successful pilot!

Once our reading of *Eyes* commenced, students completed a nightly tracker where they noted cultural, historical, sociopolitical, religious, generational, familial, and/or geographical connections between the two texts. These connections would eventually evolve into a four-paragraph compare and contrast essay.

The Assignment: Craft a multi-paragraph essay (4-5 paragraphs) that compares and/or contrasts Zora Neale Hurston's *Their Eyes Were Watching God* and Beyonce's *Lemonade*. Prior to writing, you will need to establish a clear and specific idea to explore, one that engages both *Eyes* and *Lemonade* in a profound, insightful way. Your paper should essentially explore how these texts converse with each other. Think about it like this: If *Eyes* and *Lemonade* were on a dinner date, what would they say to each other? Would they be excited to share space? Would one body of work need to express their grievances? Would they be beefing? Is it complicated? Is it a space of glorious healing or bitterness and resentment? Explore. Start by consulting your *Lemonade* trackers. Please consider the following series of questions:

How do *Eyes* and *Lemonade* work in concert to produce meaning? What do they accomplish together? What do these texts add to the discourse on Black women's lives and experiences? What do we learn by examining "old world" and "new world" narratives together? Explore.

Consider the "departures and deviations." What does *Eyes* offer that *Lemonade* doesn't (and vice versa)? Are there any points where themes, messages, and concepts diverge? Why does this happen? Does *Eyes* successfully "pass the baton?" Does *Lemonade* accept the baton and retell "the story" well? Explore.

Students ate this assignment up! Though I despise grading essays, I enjoyed reading and evaluating their assignments. Good teaching should bring joy to all parties involved.

Conclusion

To thrive in a profession that actively "spirit murders" its students and its teachers, the social justice-oriented educator must dare to create, reinvent, and dream with audacity and conviction. This is an act of rebellion. Though acting as a cultural and sociological turncoat comes with its challenges, my desire to implement humanizing educational practices and incorporate culturally relevant curriculum has yielded positive results.

Rather than reiterate the points discussed above, I'd like to conclude this chapter by sharing how my vision, my greatest asset, has affected some of the students I have taught (in other words, I'd like to substantiate the claims I've made throughout the chapter). Creation, reinvention, and radical dreaming begets increased satisfaction.

Direct Quotes From Students Describing Their Experiences With Me:

"I don't even know where to begin. You taught me more than any English teacher I've ever had IN MY LIFE. You are beyond the best teacher. You are a strong, educated, independent Black woman. I feel like when racist people make the argument that we are ghetto and uneducated, you should be the symbol that represents us, that we are not ghetto and uneducated, but that we are (Black community) strong and beautiful. You are and always will be my favorite teacher, not only because you're classy and don't let anyone bring you down, but because you taught me how to love and value others no matter who they are or where they come from. You are truly the best and you and your teacher ways will always have a place in my heart." –ZG

"What I enjoyed most about our time together was how you always pushed us to do our best, even when we didn't feel like it You truly made this group of individuals feel like one big family." – DA

"I enjoyed the project we recently did with the music album, it was so much fun. I didn't dislike anything, honestly, because English is my favorite subject and you just made it more fun. Your energy is the best, please don't lose that. And how you form connections with your students. We're all going to miss you so much. Your personality makes you a wonderful teacher." –AL

"I bloomed in this class. You did as well. You became more open and loving. You are incredible. I love you, keep growing." – Unknown

"....happiness, positivity, clarity, energy, optimism, enlightenment, remembrance, intellect, honor, loyalty and joy. These represent your teaching." –KG

"I honestly enjoyed this class every time I came here. I'm not going to lie, when you first came to this class I was a little iffy because I wanted Ms. _____ to teach. But then, I started to enjoy it and you're literally my favorite teacher in this school, even though I don't show it, I just don't like to talk. The way you interact with our class and have conversations with us makes you my favorite teacher." –DH

"You inspired me to do better and work harder." –JJ

"I want to say I enjoyed the last assignment we did together with agree and disagree because you respected and cared about our opinions and let us move around. I just wanted to say I really appreciate you and what you did for the students at our school. Not all heroes wear capes but you definitely are a hero for shaping our futures in the right way with interest and creativity. The amount of care and concern for your students is what makes you a real teacher.

Remember, when you are teaching, do you, stick with creativity and fun projects, work on patience and keep climbing those stairs to success." –RF

"Your class was very nice and relaxing. Also, it was very free where we could speak our minds and be comfortable with each other." –JS

"You're honestly one of my FAV teachers. I love your personality because you're really funny and I love how I could have a normal conversation with you like a teenager. Don't change the way you are because you're very relatable and comforting to us teens." –MM

"I liked how you related real-world situations to what we're doing or learning." –HB

"I enjoyed the lesson choices you made. I was really enthusiastic about them because I couldn't agree more with the lessons being taught, like how extracurricular activities can teach you just as much as school. I love how you make everything hip, everything from when we played "God's Plan" and "Mask Off" on the speaker while we did our work to when we watched that "thug" talk about Julius Caesar." —AR

"You made me happy. When I had bad days, you would always turn my frown upside down."

–Unknown

"I enjoyed the group work, being able to speak my mind during class and the creative learning." –SB

"I was able to trust and rely on you for anything. I love and respect you." –DS

"I love how you teach. I like when you make us think deeply." –AC

"Thank you so much for being such a wonderful teacher of English. Every day I walk into this class, I learn something new and I appreciate you for that. You are such a wonderful teacher and you make learning so much fun for us. I appreciate how open you usually are to our ideas and you are always willing to listen to what we have to say. I hope your students in Africa love you as much as we do."

–AC

"I really love the support and time you've given this class. I also really loved our last class discussion. It was "lit." –DT

"I enjoyed the projects that we did, the movies that we watched and the books that we read."

–TA

"You cared about your students and you would do anything to support them. You would have a full conversation with them." –FM

"You taught me more than just what I could read in a book.

You spread love and positivity.

This was a very black empowering environment." –OP

"I enjoyed when we had class discussions like the one about suicide because we could get our opinions out instead of writing papers or reading." –CT

"You are a teacher who makes us step out of our comfort zones. You lead us to a new world."

–Unknown

"We read a lot of great books and you taught topics that most teachers wouldn't talk about like expressing sexuality and women empowerment. Throughout the year, we had a lot of class discussions that really allowed everyone to speak their minds, even if they disagreed." –JS

"You were the first African American teacher I've had. Stay beautiful!" –NM

"I enjoyed this class a lot, it was way more fun than the rest of my classes. We always do activities and projects which are fun." –RC

"You are one of the coolest teachers I have ever met. I liked having you as a teacher because I always felt like you were one of us. We could tell you about anything." –RS

"We were all so lucky to have you as a teacher. You've made class so fun and it was different from all these other boring classes. You've taught us a lot and were such a relatable person, which I think is why I appreciate you more. Stay friendly, don't stress too much and stay humble to yourself." –BP

"We always added culture to our class." -Unknown

"I liked how we could get to put our own opinions into the discussions and I liked how we could get to talk to you about our problems when we had them." -AL

Chiara Mahogany White-Mink

Chiara is a proud graduate of Clark University in Worcester (MA) where she completed a BA degree (Cultural Studies & Communication major, English and Education minors, concentration in Comparative Race and Ethnic Studies) and earned an MA in Teaching.

After graduating with her master's degree and completing her first year of teaching in Worcester (MA), she was accepted into the United States Peace Corps and began teaching high school English in Yele Town, Sierra Leone (West Africa). Upon her return, she taught 11th Grade English (including AP English Language and Composition) at Renaissance High School in Springfield, MA; taught 9th and 10th grade English at The Loomis Chaffee School in Windsor, CT; and taught 12th grade essay classes and interview classes with American Study Education in Hanoi, Vietnam. She is currently teaching literature and TOEFL JR preparation classes at ChungDahm Academy in Anyang, South Korea. As a social justice oriented educator, she strives to teach lessons that help students move through the world more responsibly, regardless of where she is teaching.

Beyond teaching, Chiara has a penchant for writing, traveling, and reading. She is the founder of *SassyWithSubstance*, a personal development blog where she discusses topics related to self-improvement (healing), work/career, and relationships.

To date, she has traveled to twelve countries across four continents: Luxembourg, Germany, France, and England, located in Europe; Jamaica and Grenada, located in The Caribbean (North America); United Arab Emirates (Dubai) and South Korea, located in Asia; and Egypt, South Africa, Namibia, and Sierra Leone, located in Africa. Out of the 12 countries visited, she has lived and taught in three: Namibia, Southern Africa; South Korea, East Asia (current position); and Sierra Leone, West Africa. Finally, Chiara's love of reading, which developed in childhood, brings her personal fulfillment and helps her bring lessons alive in the classroom. Many of the books she brought into her classrooms, such as *The Women of Brewster Place* and *The Crossover*, were discovered simply from reading of her own volition.

Contact Information:

Email: chiarawhite25@gmail.com

Website: https://sassywithsubstance.com

Facebook: Chiara Mahogany White-Mink

Creative Leadership is Kingdom Leadership

Deborah Agbessi

Creative Leadership is Kingdom Leadership. Why? Because our heavenly Father, our Creator, is the original creator. Because we are created in His image, that also makes us creators. When we walk in our full creativity as believers, as children of the most high God, via the Holy Spirit's manifestation, we will fully know our spiritual gifts, our purpose and our calling. We can use our spiritual gifts to advance the Kingdom of God. All the more reason we should believe that we were created in God's image.

In His image, we are creators. In creative leadership, we get to use what He placed inside of us. Once we discover what that is, what our spiritual gifts are and tap into the ministry of the Holy Spirit in our lives, we can use that to tap into our creativity of being a leader here on earth. We can use Kingdom Leadership and kingdom wisdom, in how we handle our businesses and in how we handle others whom God places in our path to serve. Creative leadership can flow in and through us by the grace of God. Creative leadership helps us. God's Word shows us how to be leaders and how to be creative in our leadership.

As a Kingdom Leader, we do not operate as the world does. As a Kingdom Leader, there are things we have to adhere to according to God's Word. According to scripture, "...the Holy Spirit will guide us into all truth..." (John 16:13 King James Version). When the Holy Spirit leads us, we do things that the world does not know about and cannot comprehend. God is "...able to do exceedingly, abundantly above all that we ask or think according to His power that worketh in us." (Eph. 3:20 KJV) Therefore, by being a believer and a partner with God and the Holy Spirit, we will be able to do the things Jesus did and even greater works. (John 14:12).

A Creative Kingdom Leader has the capabilities of doing greater works. I want to expound on Kingdom Leadership and using Creative Kingdom Leadership as a method of leadership in our businesses in the world today. A majority of the multi-level network marketing business opportunities that I have experienced or been exposed to have a slogan for their compensation plan, each one get one, get two, and you are through. For some, you have to get twelve recruits. All of that, in my opinion, is a concept of how Jesus chose his followers, his disciples. He recruited them. There was something in each person's character and personality that was attractive to Jesus that caused him to say, "... *Come, follow me...*" (Matt. 4:19 KJV).

When building a team, Creative Kingdom Leadership, takes our differences in our character and personalities into consideration. One should not only look at a person's job skill set, what they can do or what they can bring to the company. One should also look at the gifts and talents that a person has that can add value to the people within a company as well as add value to the company. A job description should not be the main source in determining what a person can and cannot do for a company. Creative Kingdom Leadership is about looking beyond the natural ability of a person and looking at what they were designed or created to do. What makes them "tick"? Creative leadership, Kingdom leadership, is a spiritual thing.

The employer, leader, and hiring manager, should look beyond a person's ability to do a particular job. People can develop skill sets and be very good at what they do. However, if they do not have a deep-rooted spiritual consciousness about themselves, about who they are and how they affect people around them and what their purpose is in the earth, then that can cause them to be slow at progressing and doing their work efficiently and effectively.

In the beginning, people come off as if they can do it. They can do it all and look good. However, after the 90 days probationary period, or that one-year mark comes up, there can be a high turnover because people are not happy with their job or what they committed themselves to do. Leadership has to get more involved in finding out why their people are not happy. Some have taken surveys to assess the reason for such dissatisfaction and high turnover. Some companies have implemented Exit Interviews for this very reason.

Creative Kingdom leadership goes beyond the norm by implementing more team-focused activities and encourages people to work together, support one another, find solutions to problems and be a part of getting those solutions activated within their organization. Everyone is a valuable part of a team. It has been said, *"No man is an island."* The scripture asks us, *"Can two walk together except they be agreed?"* (Amos 3:3 KJV). If we are not in alignment with one another, how can we agree?

Creative Kingdom Leadership seeks to increase communication by getting more involved and making sure that people not only know the rules and regulations of office culture and government but also make sure that people have a personable, respectful relationship with one another. People come from many different backgrounds. Some come from backgrounds where the elders are highly respected. Some come from a background in which the way they dress is more modest. Some have more self-respect and respect for others. Creative Kingdom Leadership encourages people to respect themselves first and to respect others.

Creative Kingdom Leadership encourages people to know who they are as a person, believe in themselves, and teaches them to seek help when they need help. Creative Kingdom Leadership helps them to recognize the stress factors in their lives and redirect them to reliable resources where they can get help. Creative Kingdom Leadership involves showing compassion for others and being willing to help others; it is not a "dog eat dog" situation. In a Creative Kingdom Leadership environment, people are encouraged to be the best that they can be and to help others to be the best that they can be.

When I think about Creative Kingdom Leadership, I think about a saying from one of my mentors, John Maxwell. He says, *"People don't care how much you know until they know how much you care."* That is so true. As a Creative Kingdom Leader, we have to show compassion and love. God's Word says, *"Though I speak with the tongues of men and of angels, and have not charity, I am become as sounding brass, or a tinkling cymbal."* (1 Cor. 13:1 KJV)

You have to love yourself. It has been said, *"Hurt people hurt people, and healed people heal people."* People that are past their hurt and their pain, healed and whole, become that way because of their personal relationship with God, their self-care, and their personal development.

In their personal development, they learn how to be better leaders of themselves first, then better leaders of others. First, they have to be a creative leader of themselves. They may ask themselves, how can I improve me? We go through many trials and tribulations more than one time, more than two or three times because we have not answered the question, "How can I improve me?"

We often fail at becoming Creative Kingdom Leaders for the following reasons; not opening up our inner circle to allow others to come alongside us and walk with us, and encourage our hearts. We do not take heed to the words of wisdom they pour into us and do not have an accountability partner to help us become the leaders that God has called us to be. Many lack faith in themselves and others.

Creative Kingdom Leadership involves walking by faith. Scripture reminds us "...Faith without works is dead." (James 2:20 KJV). Our faith has to be put into action for what we are believing God for according to His Word. Most people seem to walk in their own power. The Holy Spirit does not lead them. God's Word says, "Not by might, nor by power, but by my spirit, saith the Lord of hosts." (Zech 4:6 KJV). Creative Kingdom Leadership walks by the Holy Spirit.

Check-in with the Holy Spirit often. Ask him, what am I doing today? Give me wisdom and well-balanced judgement. Pray for your enemies and your competition. Creative Kingdom Leaders are aware. They are also visionaries. They know what is going to come about. They can project situations and have answers for situations based on the Holy Spirit giving them manifested revelations from their prayer time, alone time with God and their fasting time, from their counseling sessions with their accountability partners, and from their life coaches, their mentors and the books that they read and insights that they get.

Creative Leadership, Kingdom Leadership, is a lifelong learning experience. It does not stop once you feel like you are in that leadership role. It is a lifelong journey. We are called to be examples as a Believer, as a Christian, we are called to be examples for those who are coming up behind us, for those who we are mentoring, for those who are looking up to us as leaders, whether it be in a church, a community or a business. People are always watching us, looking up to us and seeing how we are handling things.

A creative leader, who is a Believer, a Christian, a Kingdom leader, will have multiple things that we will be able to do to help show the love of God, to help minister to others and to help raise up and develop other Creative Kingdom Leaders. We have those in the Bible who have gone before us; we have Moses, Abraham, the prophets, the disciples, Jesus and the women of the Bible that have led out and been counselors and helpers and have assisted other leaders. Other leaders are not a threat to Creative Kingdom Leaders. Creative Kingdom Leaders know they can glean from other leaders. They can help each other. *"Plans go wrong for lack of advice; many advisers bring success."* Proverbs 15: 22 (New Living Translation).

When we are seeking to be the leader that God has called us to be, a person who can make a difference in our community, in the lives of others and in the organizations or anything that we are a part of, when we walk in the room, they will see the light of God upon us. They will see His glory upon us. That light makes a difference. God created that light.

When we allow our light to shine, we allow God to shine and that creative leadership, that creation, people will be able to see what God created in us. It begins to show forth outside of us. That is greater than we are. God gives the promotion. A creative Kingdom leader has to be in alignment with God and His Word.

As we align ourselves with His Word, grow in our knowledge of His Word, we begin to see that we are leaders and that we can be bold, confident and courageous leaders, knowing that our God has called us victorious. We are victorious in anything that we do. A leader walking by faith knows that, no matter what that leader comes up against, that leader will stand on the Word of God, the promises of God. *"No weapon that is formed against thee shall prosper; and every tongue that shall rise against thee in judgment thou shalt condemn. This is the heritage of the servants of the Lord, and their righteousness is of me, saith the Lord."* (Isa 54:17 KJV) Confess that word over your business, organization, your family, your friends and associates. Pray over them and cover them with the blood of Jesus. We, as Creative Kingdom Leaders, will be able to be a blessing to the world and change the world all at the same time.

Deborah Agbessi

Deborah Agbessi, aka Debbie "Jazzy" Agbessi, was born and raised in Norfolk, Virginia. She resides in South Jersey. She is an Evangelist, paralegal, writer, and personal motivator. She enjoys writing poetry, journaling, acting, speaking, emceeing, songwriting, and singing.

She serves on community entertainment committees, outreach programs, and in outreach ministries. She studies leadership at Victory In Christ Christian Center's Bible Training Center, Westville, NJ. She has studied acting at The Actor's Place, Evie Mansfield Modeling and Talent Agency, and modeling at Charm Associates, in Virginia. Debbie is a Certified John Maxwell Team Member and is Kingdom-minded.

She seeks to spread the gospel of Jesus Christ to the world, one soul at a time.

Contact Deborah at

deborahabc2015@gmail.com

deborahagbessi@hotmail.com.

Pressed But Not Crushed

Diana Sekwaila

"And the Light shines in the darkness, and the darkness has not overcome it."

~John 1: 5, Berean Literal Bible

Call the roll of life's challenges - it's inexhaustible. Even as I explore the life challenges and setbacks that I constantly suffered, I will close on the note that we're created in the image of an Overcomer and Loving Creator regardless of what we perceive him to be because of our pain, sorrows and disappointments.

Though, I was so disconsolate in the circumstances and situations that I found myself in, still, I am so grateful because I was prepared to become a creative leader who translates their broken heart into art, their pain into gain and their brokenness into greatness. Today, I am an author, mentor, faith-based life coach and conference speaker.

In this chapter, I will share with the reader my personal experience of losing my hard-earned money and wealth, how I overcame my challenges the time I was cornered and eventually creatively redirected the pressure into leadership in society.

When we find ourselves in situations of loss, we become worried about what friends, family and society will say about us. We try by all means to justify or prove to them that it is not our fault. We blame the system and everyone else to such an extent that we lose focus on who we are relative to our original design.

My hope in sharing my experience is that you will be empowered, inspired and uplifted to face this life with boldness and valor.

Background of the Story

After South Africa's 1994 first democratic election was won by the first black President, Nelson Mandela, we were all very happy and excited because human rights were enshrined in the country's constitution. Like every economically productive citizen, I relocated to the nearest city to have a taste of the urban lifestyle.

My children happened to be at multiracial school, and I was also earning well as a government employee. I was running a weekend private practice to complement my salary since I owned two houses that were both on bond.

In 1995, I became excited to find out that I was expecting a baby girl to be delivered in January 1996. I was 37 years old, a risky age to have a baby, according to medical experts. I continued taking care of my health for the sake of the safety of the baby and mine. At 32 weeks, during my normal checkup, the doctor noticed a slight increase in blood pressure without any major issues such as swollen legs, headache or dizziness to raise some concern and continuous monitoring was recommended.

Two days after the consultation, right in the middle of the night, I started feeling nauseous, followed by vomiting. I experienced sharp stomach pain and chronic back pain. All of a sudden, I was getting disorientated. I could feel myself drifting into unconsciousness. It was by God's grace that a friend staying a few kilometers away responded to my midnight call and rushed me to a hospital emergency room.

The Beginning of the Tsunami

Upon arrival at the hospital, I immediately started having seizures and a diagnosis of preeclampsia was made. I was then prepared for a caesarian section surgery to safeguard both the baby and I. We survived the surgery; the baby was put in an incubator, and she was declared to be in good health despite the fact that she was born prematurely.

I was in a coma and was not responding well to treatment. My blood pressure was uncontrollable for weeks, and I was subsequently put in High Care and ICU units, respectively. A team of nurses and doctors were around me 24/7.

The situation became worse as I kept moving in and out of consciousness. The wound was not healing, there was swelling, and the skin was becoming darker and harder. The wound was also infected with pus despite wound care management skills applied.

I was moved to ICU with the administration of postpartum treatment to prevent eclampsia, which I definitely suffered. During this time, I never saw nor held my baby since birth despite being in hospital together for two weeks. Only my husband was allowed to visit me. The isolation created more fear, worry and anxiety. The result was nothing but elevated blood pressure, which continued to frustrate the medical team. For three weeks, I stayed in the hospital for monitoring and recovery.

During most of the time I spent in the hospital, I was preoccupied by the fear of dying and leaving my children and the fear of something bad happening to my children. I worried about my finances and that I would not be able to afford my bills at the end of the month. After a good four weeks, I was discharged under strict measures of total bed rest. My blood pressure was still fluctuating based on my emotional state.

The storm

The reality was that I had started losing my other income from my weekend private practice. I had to make a decision to close the daycare center for children with intellectual disability that needed my regular intervention, which I could not do at the time. After three month's maternity leave, the only salary I was receiving was insufficient to cover all the bills.

Within four months of being unable to pay my creditors, many started the process of repossessing my goods. It started with house furniture, followed by the car. I was only able to pay for my family home as it was deducted directly from my salary.

I tried in vain to rent the other house but had tenants taking advantage of me. I tried to sell the two houses but couldn't find a buyer before they were repossessed, and we got evicted. I was forced to move out to a two-bedroom flat with six children between the ages of seventeen and a six-month-old pre-mature baby.

Our family lifestyle changed tremendously. I settled for basic food in order to make ends meet. My children started reacting negatively to the change. The older boys started hanging out late to avoid being crammed in the small flat. They also started joining the wrong company and experimenting with alcohol.

At the end of the year, I had no choice but to relocate my family to my rural village to occupy my family home. I moved in with a friend so that I could be nearer to my workplace and visit my children on a monthly basis.

It became difficult for them to adjust to the new system of education and vernacular language as the medium of instruction. They were always in trouble for disrupting classes and being involved in fights. My middle daughter became pregnant at the age of nineteen and gave birth in the middle of her matric examination season. I had to take leave to take care of her and the newly born baby to enable her to have time to prepare for her examination, which by God's grace, she eventually passed.

My middle boy joined the wrong company and dropped out of school to look for jobs. My youngest boy started drinking, dropped out of school and got involved in street fights. My oldest son continued schooling till college, got a part-time job and moved in with a friend.

Throughout all this, I had to pretend to be a strong mother and wife. In retrospect, I was negatively affected physically and emotionally. Of course, this unexpected tragic turn of events dramatically traumatized me.

I needed support, but there was no relief from the stress because my spouse was unavailable due to work reasons. He worked far away and only visited home on a monthly basis. My sickness and the loss of our home and some valuable assets drove him to overcompensate by overworking in a bid to reclaim the lost social status.

I became isolated from my friends and colleagues and became lonely and bitter too. I started to believe that maybe God was punishing me for a reason only known by Him, and felt ashamed of myself since I was failing to fit in with the standards of the academic and professional society. My self-esteem dropped drastically.

When the situation became unbearable, I relocated to a province where my husband was working with the hope that I would get some support to raise the boys, but because of his obsession with work, the boys were raised by the street.

A new struggle

This became a new dilemma for my husband, who could not live up to the expectations. He was not used to being with us daily, not used to helping with schoolwork or taking the boys out on weekends. He could not detach himself from his friends. The new life of having a family around was disruptive to his way of life away from home. There was the problem of many family challenges, and I faced the possibility of divorce daily. I became stressed, worried, and suffered insomnia.

My hubby became financially irresponsible; for instance, he created unplanned trips like visiting far away families for unexplained reasons, and attending every friend's next-of-kin funeral and wedding away from home despite our financial situation.

The situation became unbearable because sometimes we engaged in fights. The situation pushed me to the limits emotionally. I saw myself as a failure because I believed I couldn't play my role as a mother and wife. This took a toll on me physically, wherein my blood pressure kept on being elevated. I lost my appetite; even when I ate, it was just to relieve the hunger and nothing nutritional. I was prescribed some medicines to help me remain calm and sleep at night.

My struggles included but were not limited to the following:

Emotional outbursts

Anger

Worry

Anxiety

Fear

Insomnia

Loss of appetite

Sadness

Feelings of worthlessness

I started questioning God's existence.

I sought help from the wrong people.

Bitterness

Loneliness

Self-blame

One day I asked my children if they would be sad if I left home and never came back. In fact, I was checking how they would react if I were not around anymore, and this was prompted by the suicidal thoughts that had been bombarding me.

Healing and the Creative Leadership Journey

We are pressed on every side by troubles, but we are not crushed. We are perplexed, but not driven to despair. -2 Corinthians 4:8 NLT

Out of all this confusion, I applied for a new job and was hired and had to relocate to a different province. I moved away from my family, which gave me an opportunity to be alone and reflect. Later in the year, I joined a church nearby. I started joining women's ministries and activities. My house was chosen to be a cell group meeting place. In a short period of time, God started revealing himself to me in many ways.

I was given leadership positions in the women's ministry. I shared my problems with women who were mature enough to keep them confidential while praying for me. My time away from home was an opportunity to dwell in the Word of God.

I learned that God unconditionally loves us. He wants us to be fruitful and prosperous. He wants us to live a life of breakthrough. With the support of women in my church, I started declaring God's Word and His promises. I prayed for God to reveal to me who I am and my purpose on earth.

After everything that transpired in my life, with much thought and reflection, I changed my life, and today, I am the founder of *(Diana Sekwaila Restoration Foundation (DSRF)* for women and youth empowerment, a life coach and Spiritual mentor, author of three books:

Prayers that Get Answers, Experience the Personal God and *From Scrapyard to New Beginnings*. I am also a founder of *'Step Out In Love'* (*SOIL*) *Day Care* for senior citizens and the disabled and a facilitator of an online Facebook prayer for the nation; *Prayer with Diana Sekwaila*, and a founder of *Health and Wellness Community Walks*.

Diana Sekwaila

Diana is a Life Coach who uses her struggles and experiences to empower, inspire and uplift others to live a life of victory. My faith in supernatural power forms the foundational strategy of my coaching. Diana is an influential speaker on social media platforms and at seminars.

A retired Occupational Therapist having worked in both public and private sectors, her passion is helping others recover and be restored in all areas of life - physical, mental, and spiritual. Diana's clients are anyone who feels stuck and wants to get a breakthrough to their destination and live a purposeful life.

Diana authored three books: 1. *Prayers That Get Answers*; 2. *Experiencing the Personal God*; and 3. *From Scrapyard to New Beginning*. She is the CEO of *Diana Sekwaila Restoration Foundation*, an NGO where she coordinates women empowerment seminars.

A community-based health and wellness program called *Step Out In Love* (SOIL) encourages healthy living. Diana hosts a weekly live Facebook "Prayer with Diana Sekwaila," praying for the nation.

Contact Information

Email: dianasekwaila120@gmail.com

Website: https://dianasekwailaconsulting.godaddysites.com/

The Leader In Me!

Leslie Latimore-Lorfils

"The task of leadership is not to put greatness into humanity, but to elicit it, for the greatness is already there."

-John Buchan

Since I was knee-high to a grasshopper (a little girl), I always knew I was a natural-born leader with an insatiable desire to influence the masses to achieve excellence. That still rings true today!

Creativity allows you to stretch and use your imagination beyond what we will consider the regular capacity of a human being. It also opens doors to transform your mind into a space in a place of endless possibilities and opportunities.

Creative leadership is the essence of thinking entirely out of the box, reaching for higher heights and deeper depths to move your team to mission accomplishment. Sometimes it may even be considered "gaming." Creative leaders are innovative catalysts that can entice the minds of individuals and allow people to optimize their performance in unimaginable ways.

Picture the typical scenario of disgruntled employees at a workplace who have been tied to "this is how we have been doing it since 1932 (figuratively speaking) ". These individuals are resistant to change and will be the ones to go against the grain.

What is the strategy for obtaining the "buy-in" of these "not so cooperative" individuals to vote in the same direction as everyone else? Many leaders probably have faced this kind of scenario at some point.

As a military officer, I lead hundreds of people and galvanize them to accomplish a goal. As a mother of 12, I have also leveraged my ability to navigate various personalities simultaneously. I hone these critical interpersonal skills at home, in the workplace, and in any other professional environment that contains people to optimize success for everyone. It's certainly a task that takes work to achieve. However, it is essential for harmony, productivity, and mission accomplishment.

My current position entails overseeing a significant component of the Army's wounded warrior program of over 4100 members. This powerful but vital role has inherent challenges on its own. My team and I are responsible for executing regulatory guidance from our higher headquarters, including Congress. More specifically, we serve as personal assistants to individual soldiers to help them navigate what would otherwise be a complicated maze during the transition. We want to meet a need with resources and ensure that our service members receive what they are entitled to by law.

Fortunately, I have a dynamic team of individuals who understand what it is to go the extra mile and be above reproach. They all have a servant's heart to provide the premier service that our service members deserve. Our job is to ensure that they have opportunities to capitalize on all of the benefits that are available and entitled to them.

As for other leaders in my organization, there is a culture that exists that may be accustomed to the "status quo." After arriving at one of my organizations, I decided to launch a pilot program to assess every individual's leadership quality and skill set. Naturally, I decided to start with the "leaders "first.

I fully endorse the antidote of the importance of understanding how you show up and why you may show up. As a certified superpowers and behavioral specialist coach, one of 32 in the world, and the first military officer to undergo this impressive feat, I understand the importance of knowing oneself down to your DNA level.

I launched a successful pilot session, giving jaw-dropping results to my staff and teammates. As a result, I have been highly sought after to implement additional pilot sessions for other organizations. The exciting part is that it's at the grassroots level, already yielding phenomenal results!

Often, I like to infuse a little "TLC" into our ranks and organizations. (Trust, Leadership, and Cohesiveness). TLC go a long way. Let's break that down further.

T- Trust

Trust is one of the most critical pieces of any relationship, and if broken, it can lead someone into a state of devastation which can, in this way, degrade an organization.

According to Webster, trust is a firm belief in the character, ability, strength, or truth of someone or something.: a person or thing in which confidence is placed. Confidence in one's leaders will propel any organization to the next level!

L-Leadership

The definition states: The action of leading a group of people or an organization." That's how the Oxford Dictionary defines leadership. Simply put, leadership is about taking risks and challenging the status quo. Leaders motivate others to achieve something new and better.

Challenging the status quo may put you in a position that will set you apart from others in terms of making something suitable. When birthing an innovative enterprise, leaders are responsible for enforcing rules and setting conditions where the opportunity to excel is limitless.

That can also mean turning comfortable into uncomfortable, looking people in the eyes, and asking hard questions. Have you put your best foot forward, given your best, and been equitable?

And finally, C in Cohesiveness

Cohesiveness is where leaders serve as the glue and prominent link to the organization's and its people's success.

Imagine the players of LSU that experienced the incredible opportunity of winning a championship. What if one player was off-kilter because they may have been distracted by life's activities? As a creative leader, I would use this opportunity to increase my presence and availability to each player. The coaches used a similar approach, a massive catalyst to that unforgettable VICTORY.

As a leader, you are the glue to keep your team and organization together! This is done through becoming entrenched with those that work with, around, and besides you! The idea of togetherness will transcend any obstacles confronting you or your team!

If you are reading this, I want to tap into your unwavering ability to galvanize people into a realm of endless possibilities. Stop playing small and no longer accept limitations of any kind. I also would like to take it a step further for those with a disability. Your disability is not your inability to accomplish any goal or task.

Leaders are expected to be just that, LEADERS. They also have to recognize that sometimes elevation requires separation. And lastly, leaders need to tap into their creative senses to help push the organization to a new level of innovation and strategic vision.

Creative leaders are the unique interwoven pieces of fabric and exceptional life learners that create the most impressive and irreplaceable connections.

I leave you with this final quote:

Gwendolyn Brooks said, "*We are each other's harvest; we are each other's business; we are each other's magnitude and bond.*" We are a vessel for others to optimize their ability to leave an indelible mark and forever impact on others!

Philippians 4:13 also states.

I can do all things through Christ who strengthens me! My mantra for my leadership style!

Leslie Latimore-Lorfils

Leslie is a proud native of Washington, D.C., a proud and busy mother of 12 children, and is a two times #1 International and Amazon Best Selling Author. She is also a TEDx speaker.

She is an entrepreneur and the Founder and CEO of two companies; *Girl Organize That Life Productivity Coaching Program* and *Elle's Enterprises* offering business concepts and life's solutions.

Leslie is a Lieutenant Colonel in the United States Army, alongside her husband and three children. She is the Secretary and Maryland State Ambassador for Topflight Defense Inc., a nonprofit organization for female Veterans.

Additionally, Leslie has been a Delta Sigma Theta Sorority Incorporated member. Leslie is a Certified Speaker, Coach, and Trainer with the John Maxwell Leadership Team, a certified Behavioral Superpowers Specialist and Coach with *Dream Smart Academy*, and a certified online coach with the *Virtual Coach* program.

Furthermore, she is a Legal service consultant and life insurance advisor committed to helping people. Leslie enjoys teaching Zumba and Cycling, serving in her church music ministry, reading, shopping, and spending time with family and friends.

She is active in all her children's extracurricular activities, even holding a position on the school's PTA. This spirit-led woman and leader has a servant's heart and is committed to building and uplifting people, and she is Kingdom-focused.

Contact Information

Linked in http://linkedin.com/in/ltc-leslie-lorfils-8767126

FB https://www.facebook.com/Leslie.latimorelorfils

IG @ diva lorfils @ellespeakslife

Creative Women in Leadership

Atneciv Rodriguez

Did you know that women make up 51% of the population yet; they only cover a small percentage of leading positions in companies? An observation I made is that there is a global rise of women entrepreneurs in the startup era.

Women-owned business enterprises are playing a prominent role in our society. They have become a source of inspiration for other women, which in turn generates many more employment opportunities for women.

Now, imagine if more women were at the forefront of businesses- or paid the same as their counterparts. It's obvious that these gender and racial inequities harm our economy and our growth.

This is why I'm on a mission to place more women in leadership!

Women from all walks of life. Women who may be wondering, what should I do with my life, or what can I do that is more meaningful? Women who are feeling stuck? Mothers, who feel overwhelmed, have bills racking up or find it hard to get their creative ideas off the ground! Women who desire to be someone through their efforts and women who want to walk in purpose. If this is you- you're not alone. These feelings are a universal human experience. I myself experienced these sentiments.

My name is Atneciv Rodriguez, CEO & Founder of *The Leadership Center*, a Latina and woman-owned firm where I coach aspiring entrepreneurs to build, grow and sustain a powerful life and business.

I utilize equity-centered coaching to provide customized training for women who desire to take their life and business to the next level.

While there are many coaches around the world. I noticed that the consulting industry was male-dominated or with women who didn't look like me. See, I know that cultures and life/lived experiences differ, so I wanted to create a safe and inclusive space that focused on mindset, business, and finances. This way, women could really execute their passions.

As a Certified Master Life Coach (CMLC), Certified Business Consultant (CBC), Financial Licensed Advisor, Certified Practitioner in Neuro-Linguistic Programming (NLP Practitioner), former crisis advocate, and former SCORE mentor, I provide tools and education in a way that truly empowers others, because I know how to eliminate the complicated and complex through simple and direct solutions.

I've helped women who felt defeated, lost, scared, and confused with no PLAN and, within weeks, turned them into confident, self-leading, disciplined powerhouses- turning them into women who get results.

This is why I push more women towards success, pursue their passion or move into executive positions - further closing that gender and racial gap. But today, I'm going to share with you how I utilized creativity in empowering women to overcome adversities and become powerful women in leadership.

Being a woman is a challenging journey in itself, but being a woman who has faced adversities such as domestic violence, teen pregnancy, sexual abuse, and mental health issues can make the journey even more difficult. However, with a strong sense of creativity and leadership, these adversities can be transformed into opportunities for growth and empowerment, not just for oneself but for other women as well. I want to share a bit about my personal story of how I overcame these adversities and became a leading woman with a successful business by helping other women.

Growing up, I faced multiple adversities, a.k.a urban trauma, as the great Maysa Akbar names it. This shaped my life and my perspective on the world. I had experienced sexual abuse as a child at the age of 7. At the age of 16, I became pregnant with my first child; by the time I was 17, I was an emancipated mom of two. The unfortunate truth is that I had stepped into an abusive relationship.

For four years, I suffered through domestic violence and mental health issues, which only worsened after the birth of my second child. However, despite these circumstances, I knew that I had to find a way out and create a better life for myself and my children. In doing so, I left, but before I thought things would turn out for the better, my second relationship was just as abusive, if not worse.

Overcoming Adversities

The first step towards overcoming my adversities was to seek help. I reached out to organizations that provided support for victims of domestic violence and sexual abuse. Through counseling and therapy, I was able to gain a better understanding of myself and my situation. I also learned coping mechanisms that helped me deal with my mental health issues and trauma.

During this journey, I also decided to pursue my education. I wanted to give back and help other women and became an advocate for victims during my pursuit of a bachelor's degree in social science and psychology. This was a challenging journey, as I had to balance my studies with my responsibilities as a mother and as a victim of domestic violence.

By the age of 21, I was a mom of three. However, I persevered and graduated with honors. The struggle came when I had to leave. It was difficult. I found myself utilizing the same techniques I was telling the women I was working with. I had to hide it because how could I help women and not help myself? It felt like a never-ending cycle. My abusive partner had really taken control of my mind, and I thought I could never overcome my situation.

Becoming a Leader

The irony of it was that after completing my education, I decided to start my own business. It wasn't until I started personally developing, reading self-help books, and being consistent in therapy that I gained the courage and the strength to leave and never come back. With my newfound entrepreneurial journey, I wanted to create a platform that would empower women who had faced similar adversities to me.

I founded a company that provided resources and support for women who had experienced domestic violence, sexual abuse, teen pregnancy, and mental health issues. Through my company, I was able to connect with women from all over the world and provide them with the tools they needed to overcome their adversities and create a better life for themselves.

One of the key aspects of my leadership style is creativity. I believe that creativity is a powerful tool that can help us transform our adversities into opportunities. For example, I use creative techniques such as creative writing to help women express themselves and process their trauma. I also use creative marketing strategies to promote my company and reach a wider audience.

This practice led me to write in 8 different publications that led to best sellers in drama anthologies, parenting, and relationships. I've had the privilege to help and guide women in business, finances, and mindset with my creative writing, books, and courses.

Creativity leads to innovation. Being able to see the world from different perspectives and making connections between the issues and the solutions is a skill that can be developed. However, this skill requires the proper mindset. By proper, I mean a growth mindset. View your challenges not as a setback but as a learning opportunity to change the trajectory of your future. Be open to taking a risk to go after what you're passionate about.

There is nothing wrong with wanting to experiment with something that can possibly lead to a life-changing experience that you may love. The worst that can happen is it doesn't work in your favor, and you're back where you were. You really don't lose anything by trying. I've come across women who let fear take over their hearts and are not willing to think outside of the box because they allowed society to dictate what they "should" be doing rather than what they "want" to do.

Empowering Women

My company has helped thousands of women overcome their adversities and create a better life for themselves. Through resources and support, we have empowered women to become leaders in their own right. Many of our clients have gone on to start their own businesses or pursue higher education. We have also created a community of strong and supportive women who uplift and inspire each other. I am proud to say that my personal mission continues to be filled as I continue to bring more women of color into leadership. We deserve to be proud and to be seen. It takes us as leaders to continue to share, highlight and empower women to get to the next level. We have to be champions, allies, and supportive of one another. As you may know, oftentimes, it's not just what you know but who you know. So, when you're in a position to pull another woman up, do so.

Creative leadership is a powerful tool that can help us overcome adversities and empower others. Everyone has a different story and may have a different and creative way of sharing it. Through my personal journey of overcoming DV, sexual abuse, teen pregnancy, and mental health issues, I have learned that creativity and leadership go hand in hand.

By harnessing our creativity, our passion, and our purpose, we can transform our adversities into opportunities and create a better life for ourselves and others. As a leading woman of color with a successful business, I am committed to continuing to empower women and inspire them to unleash the powerful, creative leaders they are within.

Atneciv Rodriguez

Atneciv is a passionate multipreneur, who works with leaders and CEOs, executives, and solopreneurs to grow personally and professionally in business and finance and be the best advocates in their community and a change agent for women. As a voice in the female-driven movement, Atneciv continues to be a leader in the space, liberating women to trust their intuition and create their own opportunities.

She empowers clients to stop waiting for their big break and, instead, to take the leap of faith. After years of working as a community advocate, Atneciv believes that everyone has a leader within and knows what drives change and sees the needs in her community. Atneciv is now a multi-business owner of a business coaching and financial firm named *Executive Leadership*, a Spa named *BodyWaistGlam*, and a non-profit organization called *Family Leadership Center*, all centered around leadership, financial literacy, and empowerment.

Atneciv Rodriguez is a Certified Master Life Coach, Certified Business Consultant and has state and federal financial licenses with over ten years of experience. She is a 6x published author (with an upcoming book called *POWERFUL*), a confidence creator, and leader.

Her personal mission is to create more leaders. Atneciv obtained multiple degrees from the University of Bridgeport in the area of Social Science, Psychology, and Business Administration.

Contact Information

Atneciv can be reached at:

@AtnecivRodriguez.com

IG: AtnecivRodriguez

FB: ExecutiveLeadershipLLC